T0352573

Dryports – Local Solutions for Global Transport Challenges

Maritime Logistics

edited by
Frank Arendt, Hans-Dietrich Haasis
and Burkhard Lemper

Vol.6

PETER LANG

Frankfurt am Main · Berlin · Bern · Bruxelles · New York · Oxford · Wien

Manuel Kühn / Karsten Seidel /
Jochen Tholen / Günter Warsewa

Dryports – Local Solutions for Global Transport Challenges

A Study by the Institute Labour and Economy (IAW) of the University of Bremen

PETER LANG
Internationaler Verlag der Wissenschaften

Bibliographic Information published by the Deutsche Nationalbibliothek
The Deutsche Nationalbibliothek lists this publication in the Deutsche Nationalbibliografie; detailed bibliographic data is available in the internet at http://dnb.d-nb.de.

co-financed by

ISSN 1868-369X
ISBN 978-3-631-62492-0
© Peter Lang GmbH
Internationaler Verlag der Wissenschaften
Frankfurt am Main 2012
All rights reserved.

All parts of this publication are protected by copyright. Any utilisation outside the strict limits of the copyright law, without the permission of the publisher, is forbidden and liable to prosecution. This applies in particular to reproductions, translations, microfilming, and storage and processing in electronic retrieval systems.

www.peterlang.de

Empirical research requires information from various persons and institutions. We therefore would like to give sincere thanks to interview partners in administrations, associations and corporations for their openness and cooperativeness, to our project partners for valuable input and feedback, to the Dryport project management team for advice and assistance and to the European Union Interreg IVB-North Sea Region Programme as well as the German Federal Ministry of Transport, Building and Urban Development for financial support.

Manuel Kühn
Karsten Seidel
Jochen Tholen
Günter Warsewa

Table of Contents

1 Dryports - a new concept?

1.1 Global Developments

Global trade is growing, and more than 90 percent of the global trade is sea-borne trade. This requires firstly a challenge to inland logistics everywhere in the world to collect containers to be shipped and to distribute containers to be delivered to the final customers. And in order to cope with ever growing amounts of goods and containers dryports are coming up as a new hinge between inland destinations and seaports.

Increasing worldwide transport

The introduction of the container in the 1950/60s revolutionized worldwide trade. The emergence of Asia as a global economic power, the end of the cold war, innovations in information and communication technologies boosted the globalized transport further. The continuing growth of the world population and the division of labour will enhance it further.

An outlook by the Organization for Economic Co-Operation and Development (OECD) foresees a possible doubling of the worldwide GDP by 2030.[1] At the same time the maritime container traffic could grow with an annual rate of six percent. And even though GDP growth in the EU is expected to be slower than before, the OECD still sees growth rates of 1.8% per year in Europe which is about 40% from 2007-2030.

Trade growth exceeded GDP rates for many years. In the time 2000 to 2006 trade growth was twice as much as GDP. This will probably continue, even though a bit lower than before. The biggest share (in volume) in international trade is transported by sea and the fastest growing type is the shipping of containers. The container handling increased eight to ten percent annually, during the recent decades and despite a drop of ten percent in maritime container volume in 2009 due to the economic and financial crisis, the container growth is expected to continue strongly. According to the OECD, the global container handling in ports could rise up to four times the current levels until 2030 and five to six times until 2050.

Subsequent to the emergence of the container, the maritime transport needed container ships. The number of container ships worldwide grew from 10,290 in

---

1   The following forecasts are taken from: OECD (2012), Strategic Transport Infrastructure Needs to 2030, OECD Publishing. P. 29-31;
    http://dx.doi.org/10.1787/9789264114425-en.

1980 to 183,859 in 2011.[2] Simultaneously, the sizes of the vessels are also expanding. Since the 1990s the sizes grew from 4,000 TEU to 14,000 TEU. In 2013 the first ships with a container volume of 18,000 TEU will enter service for the Maersk shipping line. These ships are 400 metres long and 59 metres wide. They will probably run the most frequented intercontinental shipping routes and call only at a small number of ports that offer the required conditions in terms of draft depth, berthing lengths and extra large equipment.

The enlargement of ships will further contribute to the concentration of container traffic even more and enhance the development of the respective ports to gateways for intercontinental container traffic. Only those Mega-hubs will be able to handle high volumes of capacity, regarding space and equipment.

Just to explain this by the example of Rotterdam, which is the largest European port and had a container turnover of 11.9 million TEU in 2011: The Port of Rotterdam expects almost a tripling of volume by 2030. The container turnover is expected to rise from about 10 million TEU in 2010 to about 30 million TEU in 2030.[3] This will extremely reinforce the pressure on the already congested inland connections. One of the strategies to cope with this growing pressure is to improve the modal shift. The current rates of the different modes of transport at Rotterdam are 59 percent road, 31 percent waterway and 10 percent rail. The target rates for 2035 are 45 percent waterway, 35 percent road and 20 percent rail. Regarding the growth rates expected for that period this would mean a very strong effort.

Inland transport

The sea-borne trade with the overseas shipping lines and the feeder/short sea shipping is only one side of the world wide trade to and from the ports. On the other side is the inland transport and the capacity of inland transport infrastructures is in many cases an even bigger problem than the port capacities themselves. Where large numbers of containers arrive, there will be also large amounts of containers going inbound. Capacities in infrastructure are crucial for port competitiveness in terms of time and costs for inland transport. So, keeping the Mega-hubs functioning for an efficient cargo flow is a major challenge for the future of the international gateways and corridors. The inland connections are therefore of strategic importance.

---

2   UNCTAD statistics;
     http://unctadstat.unctad.org/TableViewer/tableView.aspx?ReportId=93.
3   Port of Rotterdam, interview 15 Dec 2010.

The OECD forecasts that "current gateway and inland transport infrastructure capacity will not be adequate to meet 2030 demand".[4] Infrastructure expansion and effective management is crucial for tackling the challenges deriving by worldwide growth. Improved efficiency of hinterland connections therefore appears a key pillar in maximising the competitiveness and success of ports in the future.

The European Commission and the OECD advise that "there needs to be a focus on strategic, multi-modal 'core networks' that can be funded and will be able to handle the major share of the future growth and transport tasks."[5] This recommendation brings in mind the question of governance. Large infrastructure developments need long-time planning and development. At the same time they have extremely high costs. Who is responsible for the investments and who will finance them? Regarding the limitation in public funds, it needs to be considered who will benefit from the infrastructures and who will take the costs for investments.

Climate change and environment

The growing container traffic will also produce additional sums of CO_2, pollute the environment and will have an impact on climate change. The international community and the European Union aim to reduce CO_2 emissions and therefore alternative modes of transport are crucial for a sustainable policy change.

Dryports

During the past decade, the concept of dryports seems to have spread throughout Europe – and it continues to gain ground. In theory, dryports appear to be one of the most appropriate answers to the challenges of economic growth and increasing amounts of cargo in European seaports: Dryports could optimise the distribution of goods by accelerating transport flows, rationalising logistics chains and improving the coordination of (traffic) infrastructures and locations. The dryport concept is considered particularly relevant to seaports, many of which are increasingly suffering from congestion, insufficient hinterland connections, lack of space for expansion and growing restrictions due to local and environmental regulations. Thus, dryports are mainly intended to support and relieve the seaports they serve.

---

4   OECD (2012), p. 22.
5   Ibid. p. 19.

So, the most relevant element of the dryport concept is the direct link to a seaport and – closely connected to that – its particular function in the logistics chain. These are also the outstanding attributes in the often cited definition(s) of dryports:

> "A dry port is an inland intermodal terminal directly connected by road or rail[6] to a seaport and operating as a centre for the transhipment of sea cargo to inland destinations. In addition to their role in cargo transhipment, dry ports may also include facilities for storage and consolidation of goods, maintenance for road or rail cargo carriers and customs clearance services. The location of these facilities at a dry port relieves competition for storage and customs space at the seaport itself."[7]

Thus far, the theory sounds excellent. In reality, however, we are confronted with a confusing variety of logistic hubs, inland terminals, distribution parks, freight villages, etc., with different characteristics and functions – and somehow connected to one or more seaports. Many of them were established during the growth period since the beginning of containerisation but only very few of them were explicitly set up as "dryports". Moreover, in many cases the creation and operation of a dryport seems to face difficulties. So, the construction of a dryport is not always the simple solution to the growth pressures faced by a seaport.

Therefore, the goal of the study is to find out how and under what conditions dryports can be successful; i.e. under what conditions dryports can work efficiently as a complementary partner for seaports and as a reasonable option for future-oriented and sustainable logistics.

---

6   Particularly in the northwest of mainland/continental Europe waterways also play an essential role in connecting a dryport with the seaport.

7   Roso, Violeta; Emergence and significance of dry ports; Report - Department of Logistics and Transportation, Chalmers University of Technology, ISSN 1652-8026, Gothenburg 2006.

1.2 Components of the Dryport Concept[8]

Spatial and environmental relief – The spatial dimension of the dryport concept

In general, dryports are seen as the combination of a certain location and a certain infrastructure – in geographical proximity to a seaport or at least with rail or waterway connections to a seaport. In this *spatial dimension*, the distance to the seaport is of relevance because it is assumed that "distant dryports", "midrange dryports" or "close-by dryports" would be suitable for a different set of functions[9]. Regardless of its distance from the seaport, the implementation and operation of a dryport always requires a large developed area equipped with appropriate infrastructures and superstructures as well as with favourable transport links not only to the seaport but also to the hinterland regions which should be connected via the dryport. So, dryports operate in a similar way to (or are) inland ports or inland distribution terminals, in order to pool traffic and hence relieve often congested road links to a seaport (most of which are found close to a large city[10]). Moreover, space for commercial operations, including logistics, is increasingly short in dense agglomerations and particularly in traditional seaport areas. Dryports are seen as a way to concentrate forwarders, warehousing, etc., in places outside or at the edges of urban areas, offering large and more concentrated freight capacities (preferably via railway) compared to individual shipping via truck.

---

8   There is a wealth of literature available, which was partially showcased during the Dryport Conference, October 20-22, 2010 in Edinburgh (see: Dryport Conference - Intermodal Strategies for Integrating Ports & Hinterlands, 21 & 22 October 2010, Balmoral Hotel, Edinburgh. Organised by SEStran and the Transport Research Institute (TRI), http://dryport-conference.tri-napier.org/) and is summarised largely in the StratMoS Work Package C report from July 2009 (The Dry Port - Concept and Perspectives, FDT- Association of Danish Transport and Logistics Centres, Main Author Lina Trainaviciute, Aalborg July 2009, 103 pages).

9   See: Roso, Violeta; Woxenius, Johan; Lumsdem, Kent; The dry port concept: connecting container seaports with the hinterland. In: Journal of Transport Geography Volume 17, Issue 5, September 2009, Pages 338-345.

10   The location of a port has been traditionally close to urban areas, as ports have their roots facilitating the waterborne leg of merchant cities. This historical pattern is changing, as can be evidenced with ports such as Zeebrugge or Bremerhaven being built in the 19th/20th century on the coast or estuary, mostly due to silting of access rivers or canals, and certainly in the 20th/21st century with ports that merely are conceived as trade hubs without their own hinterland – Gioia Tauro, Felixstowe and Wilhelmshaven, to name a few in Europe. Port extensions such as Maasvlaakte II for Rotterdam fall into the latter group as well.

And, given the fact that a dryport takes over functions of the seaport at a distant location, it could contribute to a substantial reduction of environmental problems caused by logistics operations. Following an exemplary simulation, Roso refers to the environmental benefit of "approximately 25% lower CO_2 emissions with the dryport" and approximately 2,000 road-kilometres reduced per day[11] by more concentrated/focused use of infrastructures.

Integration into the logistics chain – the functional dimension of the dryport concept

So, the location and its integration into existing transport networks are a prerequisite for the various functions a dryport could take over in logistics chains. In a *functional dimension*, dryports are a certain combination of handling and transhipment, gathering, storing, consolidating, packing, assembling and other activities, such as tax and/or customs clearance. An early UN definition from 1982, for example, defines an "inland port" as "an inland terminal to which shipping companies issue their own import B/L (Bill of Lading)[12]..." The focus on the B/L is important, as this provides a service for the shipper or consignee, eliminating the need for customs clearance in an often congested seaport.

So, the new functional quality of a dryport depends to a large extent on the availability and service range of the dryport itself (assembly, treatment, commissioning, customs clearance, etc.), its capacity to facilitate or provide the integration of goods into the logistic chain (e.g. by multimodal terminals and a high frequency of shuttle trains) and a large capacity to store, handle and forward goods (e.g. for block trains, receipt/dispatch of car carriers).

Enhancement of the seaport's competitive position – the economic dimension of the dryport concept

The kind of functions or combination of functions that are executed in a dryport finally depends on the economic purposes and goals of investors, operators and other involved actors. Hence, there is an *economic dimension* constituted by the various interests and business strategies of a sometimes wide range of private companies and public authorities. For public authorities, it might be of essential interest to support local enterprises in their logistics activities or to attract new enterprises to the region; another reason for promoting the idea of a dryport

---

11   Roso, Violeta: Emergence and Significance of Dry Ports, Presentation, Göteborg 2008-09-05, page 19.

12   UNCTAD/RDP/LDC/7, Handbook on the Management and Operation of dry ports, Geneva 1991, p. 2.

could be the expectation of economic growth, increasing numbers of jobs or tax revenues. From the perspective of the seaport, a dryport could help to overcome shortages of handling or storage capacities, save time and/or costs for the customers or improve the access to important markets in the hinterland. Some seaports in Europe, mostly on the mainland continent, are using the establishment of service offerings in the hinterland as a means to attract new customers or to offer new services to their existing clientele.

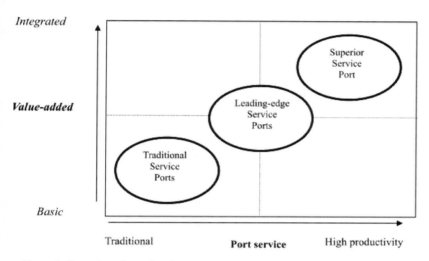

Figure 1: *Extension of port functions*

This means that the concept of dryports will only work if the concrete dryport operations are compatible with the needs of the seaport or – more exactly – of the port authority, the port operators, the logistics companies, etc.: "These days, the commercial success of a port could stem from a productivity advantage in traditional cargo-handling services, from value-added services, or from a combination of the two. Productivity advantages come mainly from economies of scale and economies of scope, suggesting that the most productive ports will be those that are equipped to handle large cargo volumes and/or significantly reduce unit costs through efficient management."[13] In order to contribute to the

---

13   UNESCAP, Transport Division, Commercial Development of Regional Ports as Logistics Centres; Bangkok 2002, p. 20.

competitive advantage[14] of the seaport in this sense, a dryport must be fully integrated into those logistics chains which are relevant for the seaport.

This basic correlation is shown in the matrix below for value-added services, but it is also true for other functions of dryports supporting the seaport[15]. As the competition between seaports in the context of globalisation seems to extend, dryports are one of the most important measures to upgrade the seaport and reconfigure its traditional logistics relations to a "superior service port" or, in other words, an "extended gateway".

1.3 Governance of Implementation and Operation

Summarising the spatial, functional and economic dimension of the dryport concept, it appears to be a win-win solution to many of today's cargo transport systems problems. Dryports can, under certain circumstances, indeed contribute to:

- Reducing environmental impacts of logistic operations;
- Relieving traffic infrastructures (particularly in dense agglomerations);
- Extending the capacities of seaports;
- Strengthening the competitive position of seaports; and
- Improving the economic structure of (peripheral) regions.

But it is also shown very clearly that there are many conditions and requirements to achieving an all-winners situation through implementing and operating a dryport. By no means can it be taken for granted that the interests of public authorities are in line with the interests of private companies, or that the expected advantages for the seaport and the seaport region are also perceived as advantages by those who want to develop the dryport location and the surrounding region. Moreover, conflicts may occur between local residents and the promoters of a dryport. This might be the case if, for example, the concrete planning and implementation of a dryport gives the impression of merely shifting problems from one place to another. Not least, there are real or potential divisions separating the interests and strategies of different involved groups of private stakeholders, i.e. port authority, terminal operators, forwarders, railroad companies, manufacturers, real estate investors/developers, etc., and some of them are even competitors.

---

14   See: Ibd., p. 21.
15   Not considered here, but also a competitive advantage can be the positioning as "green" logistics port and the environmental footprint. This was true for Zeebrugge, but in a situation of economic pressure (crisis) likely to be of less importance.

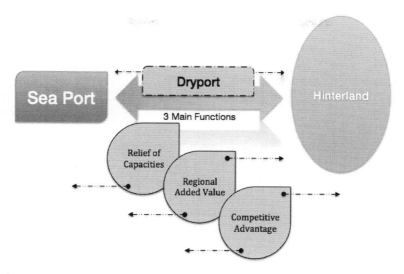

Figure 2: *Dryport functions*

Considering the complex structure of potential horizontal and vertical differences, the functional and economic integration of a certain dryport in a logistics system can only succeed if the process of planning, implementing and operating a dryport is at the same time a process of integration and coordination in a more or less complex network of stakeholders. Bridging different points of view and finding the biggest possible compromise between sometimes conflicting or diverging interests is always a challenging task and this is the core of the *governance dimension* of the dryport concept.

However, the task of network management, of coordination of different stakeholders and their interests between cooperation and competition, or of handling internal (e.g. inside a regional logistics cluster) and external (e.g. between the logistics cluster and environmentalists) conflicts is not always performed in the same way. Depending on national and regional traditions, political and economic cultures, systems of rules and regulations, and institutional arrangements, there are substantial differences. In some countries, this task of coordination is mostly left to the market (e.g. in the Anglo-Saxon countries); in some, the state and public authorities are the dominant forces (e.g. Scandinavia); and in others (e.g. Netherlands and Germany), cooperative bargaining structures form an alternative mechanism of governance. It is obvious that there will be a combination of all three governance modes in any case of dryport development, but there is always a dominant mode.

Hence, with the implementation of the governance dimension it is possible to draw a complete picture of the development of a concrete dryport. Analysing the governance dimension accounts for the functions of a certain dryport and its integration into the relevant stakeholder networks. Therefore, the differences in governance modes contribute to explain the different kinds of dryports and their different functions. Not least, it helps us to understand why certain dryports work more efficiently than others.

Given this conceptual background, the study examines the following research questions:

- What are the conditions for the specific combination of functions realised by a certain dryport?
- Under which conditions can a dryport take over an efficient relief function for one or more seaports? And, more specifically: to which sort of relief function (environmental, mitigation of capacity problems, time saving, reduction of transport corridor congestion, etc.) can dryports contribute under what conditions?
- What kind of governance mode is chosen for what reasons and how does that influence the integration of a certain dryport into a functional and stakeholder network?
- Which role plays the interrelationship between public and private actors for the governance dimension of the dryport concept?

1.4 Methodological Approach

In order to pursue the research questions, an examination was carried out under the EU's North Sea Region Interreg IVB Programme, covering case studies in four partner regions of the project "Dryport – a modal shift in practice". The enquiry was designed to compare the process of dryport implementation at Bremerhaven/Bremen, Felixstowe/Haven Gateway, Göteborg/Falköping and the Maritime Logistics Zone next to the Port of Zeebrugge. Each of these case studies represents a particular constellation of conditions for the implementation and operation of dryports and thus has allowed systematic comparison of these processes and their effects.

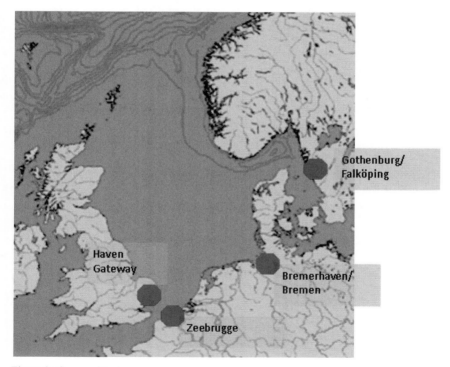

Figure 3: *Geographical coverage*

The concrete analysis work for this comparative study was undertaken during 2011, using different methods to generate and gather relevant information:

1) Appraisal of literature, conference papers, other documents and websites;
2) Questionnaires sent to the stakeholders in the case study regions;
3) Ports and dryports visited and their interrelation discussed with key stakeholders;
4) Interviews held with key actors in the regions, both from industry and public bodies. Additional background visits and interviews conducted in Amsterdam, Rotterdam and Duisburg.

The interviews as well as other information and materials were appraised and analysed according to the research issues and questions below:

	Research issue	Question for case studies
a)	Description of the specific local situation	What is the problem constellation and the problem definition?
b)	The stakeholder constellation: number and kind of actors involved; relations between relevant stakeholders	What options, interests, strategies cause what kind of relations, conflicts, cooperation etc.?
c)	Process of planning, implementing, operating the dryport	What (potential) solutions for emerging problems are found and what are their impacts/consequences (e.g. losers-winners)?
d)	Forms of governance (state/hierarchy-oriented, market/contractual-oriented, networking/ bargaining-oriented)	How do the function and the integration of the dryport correlate with the form of governance?

2 Locational Analysis: Different Condition – Different Developments

2.1 Bremerhaven – Bremen

Description and development

In this case, a particular characteristic has to be considered: The City of Bremen (about 60 kilometres south of Bremerhaven) as well as the City of Bremerhaven (directly situated at the mouth of the river Weser) are locations of seaports and both of them are run and managed by the public enterprise "Bremenports". Also, the most important stevedoring company, Eurogate, has operations at both locations. While the Ports of Bremerhaven are one of the main ports in Europe, ranking among the top five in cars and containers, the city-ports of Bremen are important for bulk and conventional cargo.

Figure 4: *Geographical location of the Bremerhaven/Bremen Extended Gateway*

So, in the City of Bremen there are two facilities that could be looked at as "Dryports". One is the Neustädter Hafen – which is not, strictly speaking, a dryport as it is a (wet) port for ships. But it does nevertheless have some characteristics of a dryport. The other dryport in our sense is the Güterverkehrszentrum (GVZ), a modern freight village where a large number of forwarders and logis tics-related companies are concentrated. This freight village is located directly adjacent to the Neustädter Hafen.

The Neustädter Hafen was set up in 1964. It was the first European container port. Neustädter Hafen was originally conceived as an overseas port in its own right to relieve the other ports of Bremen. Today, this role has changed at least with regard to container traffic because the increasing draft of ever-larger contemporary container vessels has led to access restrictions via the river Weser.

Figure 5: *Neustädter Hafen at Bremen*

The Neustädter Hafen is owned by Bremenports GmbH, a 100% subsidiary of the City of Bremen. It forms an integral part of the portfolio of Bremenports and also plays a role in the "Nationales Hafenkonzept"[16] (National Port Concept) elaborated by the German federal government in 2009.

In 1966, the first container was handled; today, the container serves as a key tool of transport in the context of multimodal logistic chains. In container logistics, Neustädter Hafen serves as a hinterland hub for the Port of Bremerhaven. Bremen-based terminal operator Eurogate uses Neustädter Hafen as an inland gateway to bring port services closer to its customers. There is a regular daily feeder

---

16   See http://www.bmvbs.de/SharedDocs/DE/Artikel/WS/nationales-hafenkonzept.html?
      linkToOverview=DE%2F Sevice%2FVolltextsuche%2Fvolltextsuche_node.html%3
      Fgtp%3D45660_list%25253D160%23id23412.

barge service between Neustädter Hafen and Bremerhaven. The distance between the two is 60 kilometres.

Currently, the Neustädter Hafen handles around 40,000 TEU per annum through its feeder barge service to Bremerhaven. This number is expected to grow significantly as the economy gradually recovers from the crisis of 2008/09.

Figure 6: *GVZ and Neustädter Hafen*

In addition to the hinterland hub function, the Neustädter Hafen also fits into the concept of a "dryport" because of its multimodal infrastructure, offering the above-mentioned shipping services as well as rail and road connections. This includes deepsea as well as shortsea, feeder and inland navigation services. Beyond this trimodal connection, there is also the Bremen City Airport, offering airfreight services.

Next to the Neustädter Hafen, there is the GVZ freight village. This is a real "dry-port" with road and rail connections. The set-up of the GVZ was the result of a process that can be traced back to an initiative of the German Ministry of Transport in the early 1960s (see article "Die Welt", 7.8.2000). The aim of this initiative was the promotion of intermodal transport, in particular via railway, to relieve roads from growing cargo traffic. Ultimately it was decided to set up the first GVZ at Bremen, with its strong logistics sector, strongly developed infrastructure and strategic hinterland position of the German seaports. The search for a suitable location was based on two key criteria; proximity to Neustädter Hafen and easy access to waterways, both inland and overseas, and railway lines already in place became the decisive arguments for the location of the GVZ. Looking back, the potential of proximity to the wet port is still not fully exploited, as there is no formal systematic cooperation in place between the GVZ and Neustädter Hafen.

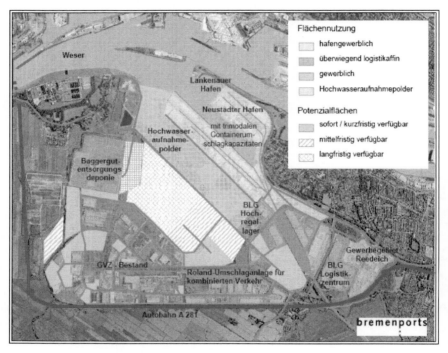

Figure 7: *Land use at GVZ and Neustädter Hafen*

The GVZ is not a legal entity in its own right but rather an area dedicated to logistics where numerous logistics companies are located. The GVZ opened in 1985 with six companies. Currently 135 companies with a total of 8,000 employees operate within the GVZ. The companies are represented in the GVZ Entwicklungsgesellschaft (GVZe), a public/private partnership of the GVZ companies and the City of Bremen.

Figure 8: *GVZ at Bremen*

The concentration of more than 130 logistics-related companies in one large area gives the opportunity to exploit some synergies; the freight village provides easy access for all resident companies to common services such as customs services, container storage areas, container repair and maintenance, truck repair and maintenance, energy supply, etc. Although the GVZ is located next to the Neustädter Hafen, there are only a few commercial or transshipment links between the two. Containers packed in the GVZ only form a minor share of containers handled in the Neustädter Hafen. The larger proportion of containers being processed in the GVZ from and to overseas destinations is forwarded by rail or road directly to Bremerhaven and Hamburg. So, the activities of the GVZ have a quadmodal potential (waterway, road, rail and airfreight) but, as water and airborne transport play a minor role, the focus is mainly on road and rail transport.

Market situation and logistic functionality

Regarding the Bremen case, a clear distinction must be made between Neustädter Hafen and the GVZ. More in-depth analysis of the function of the Neustädter Hafen shows that its "dryport character" is more or less an option for future development. Overseas services at this facility are focused on conventional cargo;

conventional cargo at Neustädter Hafen is handled by Weserport, a joint venture between Rhenus Logistics, ArcelorMittal and BLG[17].

In conventional cargo, Neustädter Hafen is a major player in its own right, not just a hinterland/feeder port. Indeed, it is the largest conventional cargo terminal in Europe. In container traffic, the Neustädter Hafen only plays a minor role but, as volumes grow in Bremerhaven, Hamburg and in particular the new deepsea Jade-Weser-Port at Wilhelmshaven, it could have the potential to accommodate additional container volumes. Feeder ships up to 5,000 TEU could in theory call at Neustädter Hafen after the planned deepening of the lower Weser.

Today, BLG operates three container gantry cranes at Neustädter Hafen[18]. Containers are currently only handled by the feeder barge service to Bremerhaven. This daily service operated by ACOS group, part of the Eurogate group, only makes up a small proportion of traffic at Neustädter Hafen. It is, though, this feature that gives Neustädter Hafen its "dryport character" – not yet its real function.

The container services at Neustädter Hafen are integrated into the Eurogate network. Currently Eurogate is contract partner for inland hubs at:

• Magdeburg, Middle-East Germany
• Minden, East Westphalia
• Dortmund, Ruhr Area
• Gernsheim, Rhein-Main Area
• Wiesau, South-East Germany
• Bremen, Neustädter Hafen

Thus the Neustädter Hafen is part of a strategic network of inland terminals which brings port services closer to customers. The overall ambition is to take the pressure off the seaports and, at the same time, improve services for the customers. This concept provides some important advantages; the capacities of existing infrastructures can be used more efficiently and the inland terminals become staging areas for hinterland transports, helping to reduce significantly storage time in the seaports.

Within this network, Neustädter Hafen stands out as it is not only a trimodal inland hub connected to rail, road and inland waterways but also an international wet port and connected to the nearby airport. Neustädter Hafen thus offers the most complete portfolio of freight and logistics services.

---

17   BLG = Bremen Logistics Group, former Bremer Lagerhaus Gesellschaft (Bremen Warehouse Company).
18   http://www.bremen-ports.de/files/2/68/101/Ports_Handbook_2009.pdf.

In relation to its feeder barge service, the Neustädter Hafen takes over distribution and packing functions in the hinterland of Bremerhaven; in the future it will do the same for Wilhelmshaven and potentially Hamburg as well. Container activities at Neustädter Hafen are operated by Eurogate. Packing services are facilitated by Dettmer Container Packing GmbH in cooperation with Eurogate. Regarding overseas destinations, Neustädter Hafen has strong links to North America, while the GVZ is handling large amounts of cargo from and to Asia. These containerised cargoes are mainly transported via Bremerhaven and Hamburg (see BLG annual report 2010, page 16).

Figure 9: *Rail connection to GVZ and Neustädter Hafen*

The GVZ operates independently from any seaport and does not have any privileged links, neither to Neustädter Hafen (although the railroad tracks connecting the Neustädter Hafen with the German railroad network cross the area of the GVZ) nor to the Port of Bremerhaven nor to any other wet port. Nevertheless, the proximity of the GVZ to Neustädter Hafen would in theory also offer some potential for closer cooperation (see ports handbook, p. 44)[19].

Despite the absence of formal cooperation between the two, the logistics companies operating from GVZ are using Neustädter Hafen on a limited scale to ship containers via the feeder barge service and Bremerhaven to overseas destinations. Therefore the GVZ is not really fulfilling a relief role for any seaport.

However, piece picking, packing, distribution and other added-value services are regular activities in freight villages like the GVZ and these activities

---

19   http://www.bremen-ports.de/files/2/68/101/Ports_Handbook_2009.pdf.

could also be taken over from seaports. So there is also a potential for relief at the GVZ, allowing the seaports to speed up their throughput of cargo, in particular containerised cargo, thus making the use of port capacities more efficient. It must be mentioned, however, that interaction between the GVZ and Neustädter Hafen as well as Bremerhaven and other ports is not yet systematically developed. But, with its intermodal rail facility "Roland Terminal" and its proximity to Neustädter Hafen as well as Bremerhaven, Hamburg and Wilhelmshaven, the GVZ does offer growth potential in the hinterland of the international ports. Logistics companies located at the GVZ are shipping some of their containers via Neustädter Hafen/Bremerhaven, but there is no formal cooperation that could facilitate these traffics on a larger scale. Bringing containers closer to customers could be an argument for "related" seaports (they are not really related yet).

Figure 10: *Rail-road combined terminal at GVZ*

In container traffic, the Neustädter Hafen facilitates feeder services for Bremerhaven, operated by ACOS group, a subsidiary of Eurogate (see ports handbook, page 52)[20]. However, these are very restricted in scale. A daily barge service carries up to 200 TEU. Even if this number is set to double due to the economic recovery, this is obviously not a significant volume with regard to relieving the Port of Bremerhaven, which handles about 5 million TEU annually. Looking at potential future developments, the Neustädter Hafen is, however,

---

20   http://www.bremenports.de/files/2/68/101/Ports_Handbook_2009.pdf.

strategically well positioned to play an important role with regard to growing container traffics in the Port of Bremerhaven. The deepening of the lower Weser will ensure that larger feeder ships up to 5,000 TEU (see ports handbook, p. 48)[21] could call at Neustädter Hafen. This is – at least in theory and possibly in future – an option for a significant relief of the large Ports of Bremerhaven and perhaps even for Hamburg and Wilhelmshaven.

The main customer target regions in the hinterland of the North German seaports are situated in Southern Germany and Central and South East Europe. In a national and European perspective, Bremen, and in particular Bremerhaven, holds a strategic position for large proportions of cargo flows transiting Germany to Central, South and South East Europe.

To maintain and even strengthen this position, ongoing extensions and improvements of transport infrastructures are considered critical. These include the deepening of the lower and outer Weser, enabling the Bremen Ports to handle larger vessels, and track improvements for hinterland rail connections to South Germany and South East Europe. Locally, the completion of the A281 motorway, including the construction of a new tunnel under the river Weser, will support the development of both the GVZ and Neustädter Hafen. All of these measures are not without controversy and a lot of conflicts are concentrated locally in the Bremen region.

---

21   http://www.bremen-ports.de/files/2/68/101/Ports_Handbook_2009.pdf.

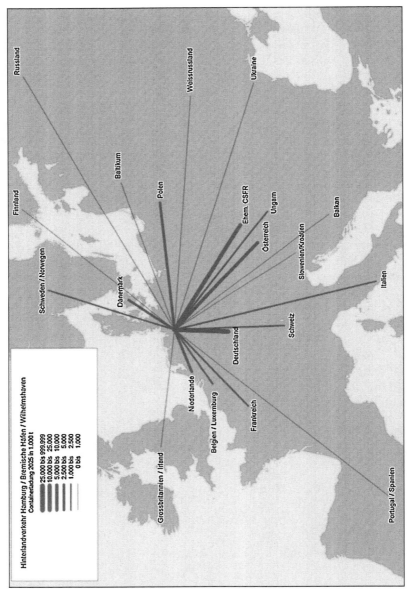

Figure 11: *Expected volumes of container traffic in 2025 from/to Hamburg/Bremen and Bremerhaven/Wilhelmshaven (in 1,000 tonnes)*

Like many others, the Ports of Bremerhaven faced a period of fast and enormous economic growth during the recent decade and although the pressure of continuous expansion has been considerably reduced because of the financial and economic crisis since 2008, it is expected that there will be an ongoing demand for expansion in the future to maintain the ports' position as a main hub for global transport flows.

In the near future, therefore, all the well-known problems of port development will return to the agenda of local and regional politics and decision-makers. There will be an ongoing need for expansion space and for dredging the river Weser, a continuous struggle with environmental activists and ecological associations, consequent conflicts with local government over infrastructure costs and traffic problems, and ongoing disputes with shipowners, railroad companies and others.

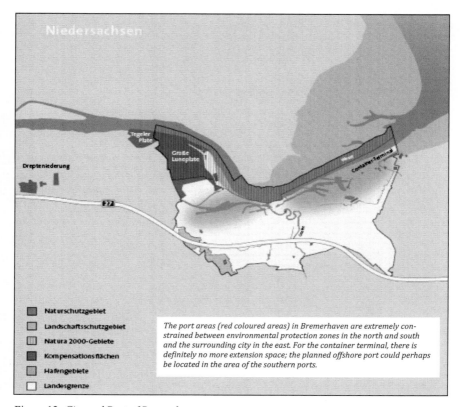

The port areas (red coloured areas) in Bremerhaven are extremely constrained between environmental protection zones in the north and south and the surrounding city in the east. For the container terminal, there is definitely no more extension space; the planned offshore port could perhaps be located in the area of the southern ports.

Figure 12: *City and Port of Bremerhaven*

The situation in Bremerhaven is characterised by various challenges:

- The ports have grown to the limits of spatial extension; being constrained by environmental protection zones in the north and south and the surrounding city in the east, there is definitively no more space for port expansion.
- Public budgets are, as a legacy of the structural crisis during the 1980s and 1990s, under extreme pressure and therefore it is doubted by many politicians and citizens whether huge amounts of investments in new port and logistic infrastructures can be accepted.
- An increasing degree of regulations and environmental constraints are leading to rising costs and prolonged planning processes for new port projects.

A large number of stakeholders - in the case of Bremerhaven, two federal states (Bundesländer), several municipalities, many environmental associations, formal and informal groups of affected residents and, of course, many different companies and associations in the port business with divergent interests - are involved in political and planning procedures, and each of them is in some way able to act as a veto-player.

Regional perspective: prospects and conflicts

Looking to the near future, the dryport's function of supporting the hinterland connections of seaports seems much more relevant in the Bremen/Bremerhaven case than its function as relief for the seaport. Today, neither the GVZ nor the Neustädter Hafen are dryports in the sense of a "functional satellite" of Bremerhaven or any other seaport. Nevertheless, in the case of the Neustädter Hafen there is potential for a strong functional connection to the container terminals at Bremerhaven, while the GVZ primarily works as a hub connecting the North German ports with important parts of their hinterland and also as a distribution centre for Northern Germany. So, the regional cluster of logistics functions can be characterised overall as an "extended gateway".

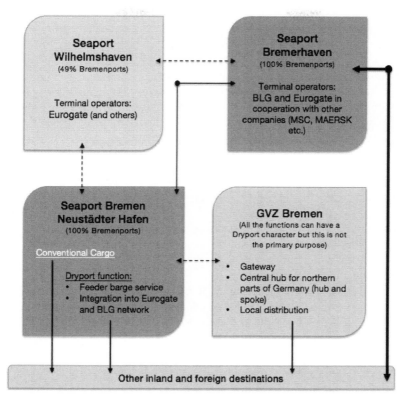

Figure 13: *Structure of the Bremerhaven/Bremen Extended Gateway*

The European mainport at Bremerhaven will in future be complemented by the new deepwater port at Wilhelmshaven, while the GVZ/Neustädter Hafen at the City of Bremen may provide the potential for spatial relief, further additional services and inland logistics functions.

The extended gateway is the core of the logistics sector and therefore it is a major economic factor in Bremen and the surrounding region. It is estimated that around 85,000 jobs within the state of Bremen depend directly or indirectly on the Ports of Bremen and Bremerhaven. This makes up roughly a quarter of all jobs – and a huge proportion of these are concentrated at the GVZ as an area dedicated to logistics with all the necessary infrastructure and services. Generally, the strength of the logistics sector in the region, combined with good infrastructure and the strong strategic position in the hinterland of Bremerhaven,

Hamburg and Wilhelmshaven seaports, makes Bremen an attractive place to invest for any logistics-related business. The success story of this attractive location for all kinds of logistics-related companies is expected to continue. Moreover, a total of 1,600 companies with about 115,000 employees across the whole region depend directly or indirectly on these ports.

These figures indicate the enormous relevance of the logistics sector for the regional labour market and for the income situation of the regional population. As logistics have always been one of the most important sectors of the economy and labour market, it is difficult to quantify the particular effects that the developments of Neustädter Hafen and the GVZ have or could have on salaries. But, regarding their key role in the development of the sector, their absence would probably mean a dramatic loss of jobs and income.

Growing cargo volumes, in particular those generated by the new Jade-Weser-Port at Wilhelmshaven and related hinterland services, promise more employment for both Bremen and the region. Neustädter Hafen and the GVZ could potentially take advantage of this development, contributing to their future development not only through growing economic success but also through creating additional jobs.

The increasing need for all kinds of staff is (as developments in the recent decade demonstrated) one of the key challenges for employers and training institutions. Modern techniques and IT solutions in logistics, increasing values, high safety standards, shorter times for handling, etc., are leading to a steady rise in the standards of qualification over the whole range of jobs in the logistics sector. To provide an appropriate workforce, employers and relevant institutions need to make jobs in the sector more attractive, and also improve the standards of training and qualification.

Despite the logistics cluster's extraordinary significance for the whole region and its economy, labour market and socio-economic structures, it seems that this cluster should optimise its performance substantially. In this way it could prepare to meet the upcoming economic challenges and fit into a more sustainable European logistics network. Taking into account the restrictions on further development, it would seem obvious that more intensive use must be made of this potential. However, this would also require a more systematic division of tasks between the individual parts of the extended gateway, as well as overcoming the restrictions which have prevented the exploitation of this potential so far. Those barriers are formed by various economic structures as well as by infrastructural deficits:

One of the very obvious problems with feeder services from the seaports to the Neustädter Hafen – and eventually from there to the GVZ – is the additional handling of containers that this requires. Containers arriving in Bremerhaven are transferred from the overseas ship to the feeder ship and then again from the feeder ship to the land transport (truck or railway). Compared to the alternative of putting containers on to truck or rail directly from the overseas vessel, these additional elements in the logistics chain obviously need more time and create extra costs. Another reason could be the profile of Neustädter Hafen as predominantly a conventional cargo port with only a minor share of container activities. Despite these difficulties, there is potential for future development of closer links between the GVZ and Neustädter Hafen.

As a matter of course, forwarders and their customers have in general no reason to take on these additional costs while there are satisfactory alternatives. But times and costs of transportation are also influenced by the entrepreneurial or functional structure of the logistics chain. If, for instance, a lot of space is required for gathering and packing huge amounts of various goods, it may be profitable to run a big warehouse at the GVZ, from which goods imported via Bremerhaven Port are distributed to many different destinations. Large shippers like, for example, Tchibo, or large forwarders such as DHL take advantage of the infrastructure and the strategic hinterland position of Bremen related to Bremerhaven or Hamburg in this way.

Directly related to this aspect is the question of the entrepreneurial structure of the logistics chain. Numerous changes of transport modes are time-consuming and cost-intensive because many different forwarders with different time schedules, IT systems, transport regulations, etc., are involved. Hence, the smart flow of goods over the entire logistics chain and the optimal integration of the seaports into this flow are of increasing importance. This is the reason why stevedoring companies, forwarders, ship owners and even port authorities increasingly look to provide the full range of supply chain services. Some of the larger port authorities (e.g. Rotterdam) "are even setting up specific development companies for this purpose"[22].

In the case of the extended gateway Bremerhaven/Bremen, this means that terminal operators at Bremerhaven (BLG or Eurogate) are also present at Neustädter Hafen and run joint ventures with different terminal operators. The most significant ones are BLG/Eurogate and Weserport GmbH. BLG activities at Neustädter Hafen are mainly focused on general cargo. In addition, BLG is operating a container terminal with three gantry cranes in partnership with Eurogate, integrating Neustädter Hafen into the Eurogate network of multimodal hinterland container transport. The containers handled at Neustädter Hafen are shipped via the feeder barge service operated by ACOS, part of the Eurogate

---

22   ESPO 2011: European Port Governance. ESPO Fact-Finding Report prepared by Patrick Verhoeven; Brussels (also available under: www.espo.be).

group. Providing the whole range of services and gaining control over the whole logistics chain is also the rationale behind BLG starting to operate its own rail connections to strategic hinterland destinations and Eurogate participating as a stakeholder in some inland hubs (see above).

So, the question of strategic control over logistics chains and networks is a matter of strong competition between transport modes and big players in logistics all over Europe. However, the further optimisation of logistic chains – and in particular its orientation towards a more sustainable development – would probably require more strategic cooperation rather than competition between different transport modes and logistic companies. In this way, the quadmodality together with the strategic hinterland position related to Bremerhaven, Hamburg and Wilhelmshaven creates future growth potential for the Neustädter Hafen and the GVZ at Bremen. Eurogate is incorporating Neustädter Hafen in its long-term strategic planning to ease the pressure on its seaport terminals and with a view to getting closer to its customers[23]. So, strengthening the dryport function of the Neustädter Hafen could in future become a realistic option. However, a stronger employment of Neustädter Hafen as well as the GVZ would require resolving some infrastructural problems, too.

An outstanding feature of the Bremen case is the quadmodal connection including the City Airport of Bremen within 6 kilometres of the GVZ and Neustädter Hafen. So far, the potential of the quadmodality and the proximity of Neustädter Hafen and the GVZ is not fully exploited. There is, though, the political will to develop stronger intermodality of cargo traffics from, to and through Bremen, building on this potential.

The most important infrastructure investment is actually the construction of the Jade-Weser-Port at Wilhelmshaven. This new deepsea port is a shared investment by the Bundesland Bremen and the Bundesland Lower Saxony and will start operating in 2012. It is expected to attract more containerised cargo to the region but this will create further infrastructure requirements. Road and rail connections from Wilhelmshaven to the South need to be widened substantially. In particular, the capacity of the rail tracks crossing the City of Oldenburg and the City of Bremen are not sufficient for handling additional cargo trains. In contrast to the Neustädter Hafen in Bremen, there is no adequate connection to the inland waterways system from Wilhelmshaven.

Both Neustädter Hafen and the GVZ are connected via rail and road and Neustädter Hafen is additionally offering regular feeder barge services for containers from and to Bremerhaven. This barge service could easily be extended if

---

23   http://www.hafen-hamburg.de/content/eurogate-baut-inland-containerterminal-
      netzwerk-auf.

it appeared necessary. Also, the connections to the German inland waterways network are in good condition.

Dredging the lower Weser would allow larger feeder vessels to call at Neustädter Hafen but the potential of 4,000-5,000 TEU feeder ships calling Bremen is unclear. In any case, a much stronger use of the Neustädter Hafen would cause further environmental problems with the neighbouring residential areas. Additional costs for light, pollution and noise protection must be taken into account.

Similar problems are also foreseen if rail connections are extended. Currently most container and car-carrying trains have to cross the inner city of Bremen and pass through the central station of Bremen. Apart from the infrastructure developments in the City of Bremen, one of the most relevant bottlenecks is the southbound rail connections. Various solutions (for example, a new Y-track between Bremen, Hamburg and Hannover) are in discussion but it is not yet decided how, when and where a more efficient rail connection will be built.

A core element of the development of the GVZ and Neustädter Hafen is the completion of the motorway ringroad around Bremen, connecting the A1 and A27 motorways via the new A281. This ringroad will allow an important improvement in the efficiency of cargo traffic flows from and to Bremen, shortening travel time from and to Bremerhaven (A27), Hamburg (A1), Ruhr area (A1) and Hannover (A7 via A27).

Finally, this ring-road connecting the GVZ, the Neustädter Hafen and the airport with the peripheral highways in the north and south of Bremen will take another couple of years to complete. The project involves some extremely long and complicated planning processes and political discussions because some parts of the motorway pass residential as well as environmentally protected areas and a remarkable number of citizens living near the planned route of the A281 are affected. This project has been highly controversial and opposed by different groups of citizens. Growing traffic volumes can reduce quality of life as well as the value of private homes. Therefore every single part of the motorway construction is or was met by strong resistance.

A more general issue regarding infrastructure developments is the requirement to set up ecological compensation areas. As there is so far no shortage of suitable land for this purpose, there are currently no significant conflicts.

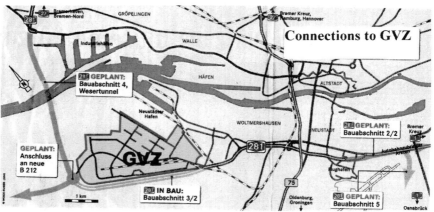

Figure 14: *Road connections for GVZ under construction or in planning*

Governance

In a more comprehensive view, the current situation and the upcoming developments are characterised by a strategic dilemma. In order to enhance and even to maintain the economic performance of the extended gateway Bremerhaven/Bremen (and, in the future, combined with Wilhelmshaven), the gateway must extend its logistics capacities to cope with growing amounts of cargo. In particular, there is a need for spatial expansion (for this, a variety of options is available and it will depend on economical and political decisions as to which location is chosen for additional logistics activities) and for large infrastructural investments (which require difficult agreements about cost-sharing between private companies, the Deutsche Bahn and public bodies on a regional and national level).

On the other hand, however, it is vital to avoid too much "growth stress". Plans and decisions must take into account the different and often competing interests of private companies as well as the concerns of residents, environmentalists and others. Not least, regional developments must be coordinated with national and supranational strategies – e.g. the European Green Corridor concept, the German government's transport infrastructure plans, etc.

Obviously, a balanced development reflecting all of these facts and interests is primarily a governance problem. So, in the case of Bremerhaven/Bremen the question of what benefits could be generated by a dryport leads to the question of how the partly conflicting, partly divergent requirements of developing a regional logistics cluster could efficiently be governed. The analysis of this case reveals two major preconditions for an efficient and future-oriented governance:

- Political leadership and the capability to act for governmental and public institutions; and
- An adequate balance of competition and cooperation between the different actors involved.
- Both Neustädter Hafen and the GVZ are characterised by cooperation between public and private entities. Neustädter Hafen is owned by Bremenports GmbH, a 100% subsidiary of the City of Bremen. Terminal operations and other services are partly run by private companies but partly also by BLG and Eurogate, which are public/private partnerships. BLG is owned by the City of Bremen, the Bremer Landesbank, the Sparkasse Bremen and various smaller private shareholders. Eurogate is a joint venture of BLG and Hamburg-based Eurokai, a privately owned terminal operator.

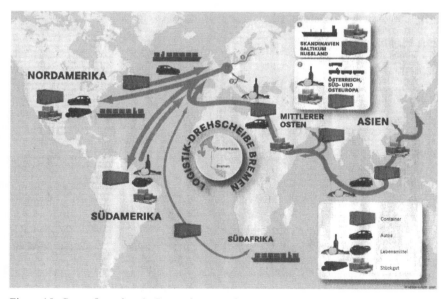

Figure 15: *Cargo flows from/to Bremerhaven and Bremen*

With Eurogate, in addition to public and private interests, the relation between Bremen and Hamburg plays a significant role. Container terminals at Hamburg and Bremerhaven as well as at the new Jade-Weser-Port at Wilhelmshaven are or will be operated by Eurogate. Competition between Bremen and Hamburg is gradually making way for a cooperation approach, securing competitiveness on the global market and against the ports of the ZARA range.

Enforcing the position of the Bremerhaven/Bremen extended gateway in this competitive environment is a major goal of governmental politics and in recent times this has included organising an intensified collaboration in the region and with Hamburg.

In fact, corporatisation of the Bremen Port Authority and the public stevedoring company BLG has intentionally transformed these organisations into market-oriented companies. Following their corporatisation, both BLG (BLG Logistics Group AG & Co. KG) and Bremenports GmbH & Co. KG, no longer work as instruments for steering and regulating under direct political control. Nevertheless, their overall business strategies and big investments – like, for instance, the decision to take part in developing the Jade-Weser-Port at Wilhelmshaven – need to be agreed with the government of the Bundesland Bremen, which is a 100% owner of both companies. So, there is a certain political influence via Bremenports and BLG on port development and also on the regional logistics cluster, because together with their numerous subsidiary and affiliated companies they are the most important players in this area.

There may, however, be contradictions, because these powerful actors are always involved in any relevant political processes and decisions, but in most cases the political goals of the Bremen government are in line with the business interests and decisions of its own companies. The container terminal operator Eurogate, for example, is partly owned by Bremen via BLG. In this constellation, the economic interest of the company (maximising profit) is mixed up with local and regional political interests (keeping/attracting cargo volume in the region to create jobs and generate tax revenue). Because of the strong strategic position of Bremen in the hinterland of Bremerhaven, Hamburg and Wilhelmshaven, these two aims are converging to a large extent; logistics are important for Bremen, but Bremen is also important for logistics.

Besides the publicly owned companies, there are other instruments for political influence but these tools are of limited efficiency. The ownership of the land and the financial investments in infrastructures are generally used in a way that primarily supports the competitive position of the extended gateway. In return, there are rewards for the City of Bremen in terms of growth, jobs and tax revenues. As logistics companies are strongly benefiting from the quadmodal infrastructure and the strategic hinterland position of Bremen in relation to the seaports of Bremerhaven, Hamburg and Wilhelmshaven, it can be assumed that the current developments have the character of a win-win situation. The drivers of the GVZ development are the companies operating it in close cooperation with the City of Bremen, and the seaports are not directly taking any stake in it. The institutional backbone of the GVZ freight village is the GVZ Entwicklungsgesellschaft (GVZe), a public/private partnership of the companies within the

GVZ and the City of Bremen, which holds 25% of the GVZe shares, securing some influence in the future development of the GVZ.

This partnership has two important functions:

- The concept of the GVZ freight village includes generating synergies through joint activities by the companies involved. These include joint purchasing of, for example, energy and telecommunication services, and joint use of storage space, service facilities and infrastructure (customs services, container repair, storage and maintenance, intermodal rail/road terminal, etc.). GVZe is the tool required to organise these collaborative features. Moreover, there is no unified landlord at the GVZ. Private companies and the City of Bremen share the costs of promotion, political lobbying and centralised services by GVZe. In return, companies take advantage of the infrastructure and the organisational framework of the GVZ.
- So, as a public/private partnership, GVZe also works as a clearing mechanism for public and private interests and this helps to find agreements about how to share the risks and costs of investments and jointly used infrastructure.

Logistics is obviously a major factor in the local/regional economy. Securing sustainable competitiveness of the logistics sector is therefore a core priority of Bremen economic policy. Nevertheless, there is an explicit political objective to support all efforts for "green logistics" and to promote the ecological sustainability of logistic operations. Both Neustädter Hafen and the GVZ contribute to the positive environmental impact of intermodal logistics chains by creating new opportunities for an extended use of rail and waterways and thus reducing CO_2 emissions. But again, in many cases this requires large investments in modern infrastructure for intermodal logistics and this is always a question of cost sharing between the local government and other (private) partners.

While owning the land and having statutory responsibility for spatial planning and environmental and other legislation, the City of Bremen could also use these instruments to influence the development of the logistics cluster. This is particularly relevant in the case of the GVZ, because there are no large expansion plans at the Neustädter Hafen in the near future. In contrast, 276 hectares is earmarked for the extension of the GVZ. The preparation of these areas for industrial use requires, according to environmental legislation, ecological compensation, which is mandatory for any major infrastructure development. This compensation is provided by renaturation of mostly agricultural land, creating ecologically valuable habitats for flora and fauna. It is estimated that the average share of investment for ecological compensation is about 10% of the entire costs.

The development of the regional logistics cluster can to a certain extent be influenced by political willingness and the use of those instruments at the disposal of government and administration. But the Bremerhaven/Bremen extended gateway is a very complex network of different actors and interests – in fact, it is a melange of at least two networks. The intentional integration of a dryport into this complex constellation or a systematic division of tasks and functions within this constellation cannot be implemented by "control and command"; it requires a high degree of coordination and agreement. So, if a dryport is to be dedicated to the specific function of physical and environmental relief of the seaport, this must be arranged and agreed within the entire network. Hence it is much easier to implement this function if the internal relationships have a cooperative nature rather than being highly competitive. Similar to the Zeebrugge case, the horizontal or dynamic network exchange ultimately "regulates" the development of the regional logistics cluster.

Both the GVZ and the Neustädter Hafen are characterised by cooperation and network relationships between public and private entities, but in different ways and with a different background and history. While the companies and institutions operating at the Neustädter Hafen are involved in a regional "port community" and in this way also socially connected to the port operators at Bremerhaven, the logistics companies and institutions at the GVZ form a separate "logistics community" together with other firms and actors in the region. As a matter of course there is a large intersection between both networks, but neither the constellation of involved players nor the interests are identical.

In addition to Bremenports, BLG and Eurogate, and their subsidiaries, a number of other private companies are operating at the Neustädter Hafen. Weserport is a joint venture of Rhenus and ArcelorMittal, mainly focused on general and bulk cargo. General and heavy cargos are the only goods handled by Weserport at Neustädter Hafen; the company is active in container handling too, but at the Industriehafen, another port in the City of Bremen. Container packing services at the Neustädter Hafen are operated by Dettmer Container Packing GmbH in cooperation with BLG/Eurogate. Other container services such as repair, maintenance, cleaning, etc., are offered by Remain GmbH, a subsidiary of Eurogate.

When it comes to the line-up of actors at the GVZ, it is obvious that the constellation is much more diverse. Besides the large number of logistics companies and the relevant parts of the public administration, there are many other important players, e.g. some big project developers specialising in warehousing, distribution parks or other real estate projects in logistics. Like forwarders and other companies in the GVZ, these project developers are operating on a national or international level. Amongst others, BLG is also represented at the

GVZ, operating Europe's largest high-stacking warehouse. Other major players within the GVZ include Deutsche Bahn and DHL. The GVZ is not a unified legal entity and therefore does not have a landlord. Rather, it is an area dedicated to the logistics activities of private companies. The land is owned by the respective companies. Unlike most seaports, the GVZ therefore does not have a "port authority" that decides on land lease, infrastructure development and general regulations for operations. Coordination of the GVZ activities works as a horizontal network. Public interest is represented in GVZe by the City of Bremen, but no direct public authority is executed. GVZe is not strictly speaking a "port authority" but a coordinating and lobbying institution of the companies involved in the GVZ. The assembly of stakeholders elects an executive board for the management of all kinds of common affairs.

One of the most significant intersections between the "port community" and the "logistics community" is formed by various transport companies. In the context of intermodal container logistics, there are several cooperations in place at Bremen. NTT 2000 (Neutral Triangle Train) is a joint venture of Eurogate, ACOS (which also belongs to Eurogate), EVB and Rhenus. NTT 2000 operates container rail services between the ports of Hamburg, Bremerhaven and Bremen. NeCoss is another rail joint venture, owned by EVB, ACOS, Rhenus and Connex. NeCoss operates hinterland connections from Roland Terminal at the GVZ to various destinations in Germany. The services of NTT 2000 and Ne-Coss meet at Roland Terminal/the GVZ. Thus they jointly facilitate the connection between the seaports and hinterland destinations.

So, the structure of the "port community" seems more homogeneous and transparent than the "logistics community"; the port community network includes the relevant players from Bremen and Bremerhaven and the influence of governmental politics may be bigger, because of the leading role of the publicly owned companies. As a matter of course, this network has also built some institutional mechanisms to facilitate cooperation and joint representation of interests.

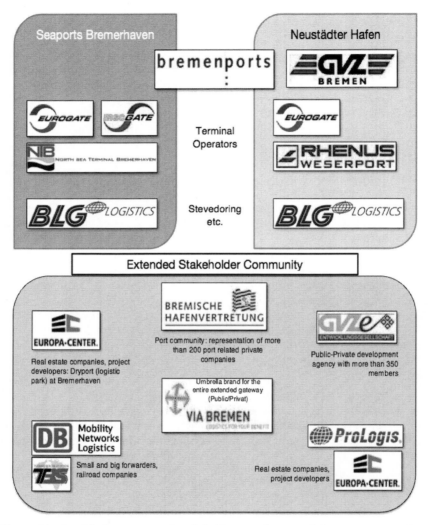

Figure 16: *Simplified structure of stakeholders in the extended gateway network at Bremerhaven/Bremen*

Taking into account the large diversity of actors and interests in the "logistics community", it is even more important that there are such mechanisms for common representation and organising cooperation. The most important of these instruments is GVZe, which coordinates the GVZ operations.

In addition to this and to lobby and promote the concept of freight villages on a national and international level, the Deutsche GVZ Gesellschaft (German GVZ Society, DGG) was set up in 1993. As Bremen was the location of the first GVZ, DGG also chose Bremen as its headquarters. The shareholders of DGG are ISL and LUB Consulting GmbH. The activities of DGG are centred on the transregional cooperation of all German freight villages. Core areas of cooperation are:

• Setting up of a logistics-oriented service portfolio at the freight villages;
• Realising intermodal transport relations between freight villages;
• Intensifying location marketing and harmonising of service standards;
• Developing sustainable models for organising institutions for the development and operation of freight villages[24].

As an umbrella over the port activities in a narrow sense and the logistics activities in a more general sense, logistics activities in Bremen are collectively marketed under the VIA Bremen brand. The private companies of the logistics sector are organised in this network, as well as the port community and the chambers of commerce of Bremen and Bremerhaven. While private companies are all represented by their regional umbrella associations, the public companies Bremenports and BLG, the Ministry for Economy, Labour and Ports and the public Economic Development Agency are single members of VIA Bremen. The aim of this new brand is to generate synergies and develop the regional logistics cluster as a comprehensive logistics centre offering a full range of services at a strategically well-positioned location. This underpins the important role that logistics play in the economic policy of Bremen.

The VIA Bremen branding represents a concerted effort to promote logistics activities at Bremen. All available capacities and infrastructures are presented as one integrated intermodal logistics hub. These include the full portfolio of overseas services, inland navigation, shortsea shipping, and rail, road and air transport. So, the implementation of VIA Bremen translates the idea of better cooperation and coordination of activities into reality. VIA Bremen strives to bring together as many players in the port and logistics industries as possible and to bundle their logistics competencies in a continuous process of innovation, with the ultimate goal of maximising customer benefit.

---

24   http://www.the GVZ-org.de/index.php?id=48&no_cache=1.

In order to carry out these activities, VIA Bremen takes on the central role as a neutral coordination, information and communications platform for the port and logistics centre Bremen/Bremerhaven:

• Representation of the ports and logistics industry;
• Coordination of ports and logistics marketing;
• Tapping into productivity and bundling potential;
• Cooperation with training and development facilities and research institutes.[25]

Conclusions

The implementation of 'VIA Bremen' demonstrates very clearly that the requirement for more intensive communication, cooperation and coordination between public and private actors is well understood in the Bremen region. So far the conditions for the extension of dryport functions are rather good:

1) with the Neustädter Hafen and the GVZ (including existing expansion space), there is an excellent potential for dryport operations;
2) all of the involved private and public companies and institutions increasingly understand that they can meet future challenges more successfully if they are acting as the extended gateway Bremerhaven/Bremen rather than as a conglomerate of diverse – and sometimes even competing – players and interests;
3) some networking tools and mechanisms for efficient coordination and regulation of the activities of the logistic cluster do exist and could support internal arrangements concerning the division of tasks between different locations and actors as well as the extension of dryport functions.

So, the stage is set – but in reality, making use of the opportunities will depend on economic development and business calculations. More investments in dryport activities will not happen before there is the expectation of a clear benefit for a majority of the participants in the existing networks. Beyond the governance problem of organising this kind of agreement, there is finally another problem, which is particularly highlighted by the significant controversy over the A281 motorway in Bremen. Agreements between private economic companies and public institutions often do not take into account the interests of residents and other stakeholders. In some cases this leads to uncomfortable difficulties and delays, but the Bremerhaven/Bremen case also shows that more participation and involvement of the resident population increases the imponderabilities of such processes and makes governance problems even more complex.

---

25   http://www.via-bremen.com/58_2.

2.2 Göteborg – Falköping

Description and development

The Skaraborg dryport in Falköping was built in 2006. The container terminal extends over three hectares and the associated logistics park has another 70 hectares.

In 2006 the container terminal Skaraborg/Falköping became part of the Port of Gothenburg's Railport network, which consists of 24 inland terminals linked by rail shuttle to the seaport. However, in 2008, because of the global financial and economic crisis, the shuttle train between Skaraborg/Falköping and Gothenburg was ceased. In July 2011, the container terminal operations of Skaraborg were taken over by TBN Akeri AB, a logistics operator for trucks. Nevertheless, the container turnover is still limited and, at the moment, the economic basis for Skaraborg is largely centred on the timber business.

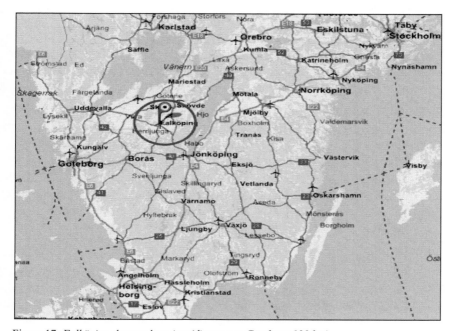

Figure 17: *Falköping dryport location (distance to Göteborg 120 km)*

Skaraborg has a new, purpose-built forest products terminal. The operator, Stora Enso, uses the facility as a hub, bringing in timber by rail from Western Sweden and then delivering it to its paper mills and plants in Mid Sweden. The finished paper is later exported, much of it through the seaport of Gothenburg.

The Port of Gothenburg is 100% owned by the municipality of Gothenburg and is the largest port in Scandinavia, with a volume of 880,000 containers per year (2010). About 50% of the containers are going out by rail. The main target regions are South and Mid Sweden and South Norway, including the Oslo region. The Port of Gothenburg is about 120 kilometres from Falköping.

In 2009, the City of Gothenburg, as the only owner, decided that the activities of the port would be divided into a port authority with responsibility for the infrastructure and three terminal operators for the container, roll-on/roll-off and car terminals respectively. In February 2010, Skandia Container Terminal AB, a newly formed corporation demerged from the Port of Gothenburg and still owned by the city of Gothenburg, took over the operation of the container terminal at the Port of Gothenburg. The container terminal was contracted to APM Terminals (APMT) in September 2011. APMT is a subsidiary of the Danish-based A.P. Moller-Maersk Group. At the moment it is not clear how the new container terminal operator at the Port of Gothenburg will continue the inland business strategy related to the Railport network. However, APMT has already announced that it will expand the rail track infrastructure inside the port.

Function and market situation

The Port of Gothenburg owns and promotes its Railport concept, and has continued to do so since APMT took over the container terminal. This concept integrates inland terminals (see picture below) in the marketing strategy of the Port of Gothenburg. It promotes intermodal transport with environmental benefits. The customs, storage, etc., could be handled at the inland terminals. The Port of Gothenburg developed the concept and the integrated marketing campaign and receives in return 5% to 70% of revenues for containers in a dryport. The port negotiates the conditions individually with the dryport operators. Accordingly, the main competition is among the dryports.

Regarding the market situation, the dryport depends on the seaport for shuttles with larger imports/exports of goods. The Port of Gothenburg is the main seaport and has no serious competitor either in Sweden or in Scandinavia regarding larger container volumes. The share of Gothenburg's container volume in Sweden is estimated to be about 60%.

The Port of Gothenburg has 24 active rail shuttles (2010) managed by nine companies heading to 22 railports in Sweden and Norway. In 2000, there were only five train shuttles. After the 2001 privatisation of Green Cargo, the national logistics company for rail transport, several private truck companies also started to operate rail shuttles. The Port of Gothenburg owns the rail terminal and offers slots for rail shuttles. Its terminals are open for any customer. However, the port has not made major investments and has not taken responsibility or risks in hinterland development. A function of Skaraborg as an external hub for the Port of Gothenburg is possible, but its realisation depends on the strategy of the future operator of the seaport terminal.

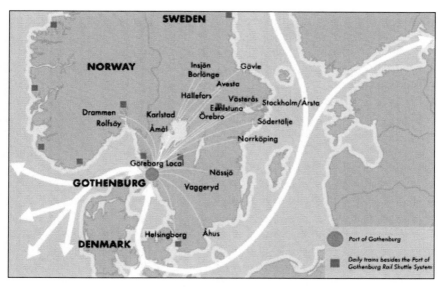

Figure 18: *Railport network of the Port of Gothenburg*

Falköping is located in a competitive road distance from the seaport. A location nearer to the seaport is virtually impossible, because land is not available. The dryport is located between Stockholm and Gothenburg and the target region is Central Sweden. The Skaraborg dryport could be used as a location for distribution and packing for Central Sweden. The main private investors in the dryport are Stora Enso for timber processing and TBN Akeri AB, as terminal operator, which handles the container traffic in Falköping. The industry around the dryport is just starting to become active. The municipality of Falköping is trying to attract businesses to invest in the dryport facilities. The activities related to the timber terminals have increased recently and there are now three to four companies using Falköping for timber transport operations. The traffic average is about one-and-a-half trains per day.

The connection between Skaraborg and Gothenburg seaport is still very loose. A frequent rail shuttle is not yet running but rail links to the main line were established in 2011. The Port of Gothenburg has no space problem, so a mere container depot is not an option at the moment. Therefore, the dryport in Falköping is at present not part of the seaport's growth strategy. However, it could be used as a more efficient shuttle destination, with more frequently running fully loaded trains, if there were to be sufficient container volumes in the future.

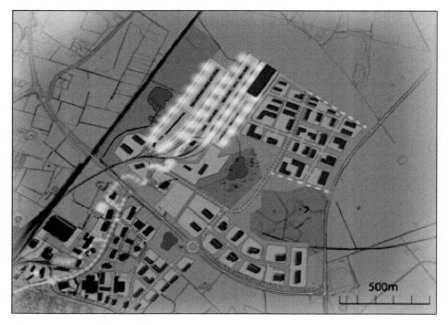

Figure 19: *Dryport Skaraborg in Falköping*

The Port of Gothenburg is trying to expand its hinterland outreach to the whole of Scandinavia and the Baltic countries. It is also considering its involvement in five or six strategic inland terminals in the future, but what the cooperation would look like or who would run the dryports has not been specified. The port has owned a 20% share in Gävle, a container port north of Stockholm, since 2005.

Looking ahead, Skaraborg might not totally depend on the seaport in Gothenburg for its export businesses. There are road and rail constraints to continental Europe in the South of Sweden and in Denmark. A new connection to Germany could help to ease bottlenecks, and to foster competition; a Fehmarn Belt bridge is planned to be finished by 2020 and would reduce road and rail distances between Hamburg and Sweden via Denmark by 160 kilometres. It is conceivable that this development would lead to more cargo going via the Port of Hamburg, due to its closer proximity. Skaraborg could act as a dryport for container traffic between Mid Sweden and Hamburg. This could stimulate competition with the Port of Gothenburg.

Due to its location in Central Sweden, Skaraborg has the potential to operate as an extended gateway for a seaport or for a distribution/packing centre. The selling point is the location next to the railway line between Gothenburg and Stockholm. At the same time, there is a strong support from the municipality of Falköping.

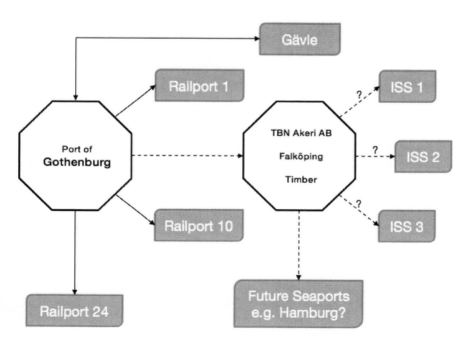

Figure 20: *Competition or Cooperation? – Port of Gothenburg and Skaraborg/Falköping*

Governance

The landlord of the dryport is the municipality of Falköping. The municipality provides rail and road infrastructure, water and drainage services. The terminal operations are private and conducted by private stakeholders on infrastructure owned and operated by the municipality. All activities of the dryport are market-based on the joint platform "Skaraborg Logistic Centre". The main driving force for Skaraborg is the municipality of Falköping, which has actively worked on the development of a dryport in Skaraborg for a substantial period of time.

The development process of Skaraborg has been conducted in close collaboration with academia, especially with Gothenburg School of Business, Economics and Law at Gothenburg University and Chalmers University of Technology. Other important actors involved in the development process were and are the Swedish Road Authority, Swedish Rail Authority (merged to become the Swedish Transport Administration in 2010), the Port of Gothenburg, Region Västra Götaland and local and regional businesses.

Public rail and road infrastructure and water and drainage solutions have been developed in collaboration with rail and road authorities.

TBN Aker AB, a Falköping-based logistics company for trucks, took over the container terminal in July 2011 from ISS TraffiCare AB, having been a subcontractor for two years. In Sweden, ISS, among others, operates inland terminals in Umeå, Jönköping and Stockholm. The container terminal in Falköping was developed in a close collaboration between TBN and ISS from July 2009. This was part of ISS's strategy to develop new business areas related to ports and terminals. The ISS inland network could be used for container movements in the future. For import/export of containers, there is a dependency on the Port of Gothenburg.

The new round timber terminal was established and financed by Stora Enso Forest AB, and started operations in November 2010. In parallel, the municipality of Falköping has built a rail link to the exchange yard. The timber terminal and the exchange yard, together with the connecting line, create the physical prerequisites for the development of the dryport and its connecting logistics park. The ambition is to be able to establish the new terminal, including the dryport concept, in 2012.

The major rail freight company is Green Cargo, which was privatised in 2001 but remained 100% state-owned. Green Cargo only conducts rail transport. For road transport, partners in the haulage sector are needed. These logistics companies also started to run railway shuttles and to become terminal operators in the past ten years. However, the rail shuttles from and to the Port of Gothenburg ceased during the recent economic crisis.

The Region Västra Götaland, in which Falköping and the Port of Gothenburg are located, sees the development of the dryport in Falköping as a pilot project and has helped in promoting it – for example, in public relations.

In the process of the dryport development, there was competition between different municipalities in Västra Götaland. The municipality of neighbouring Skövde, which has a production site for the car and truck producer Volvo, competed with Falköping on the development of a dryport. Other municipalities have an influence over railway tracks running through their areas. For instance, the subregion Laerm, between Gothenburg and Falköping, vetoed a rail infrastructure project on the Gothenburg-Stockholm line. Therefore double-tracking was not possible there.

The Port of Gothenburg was not the driving force for the dryport development in Skaraborg, but a public/private partner expressing interest in collaboration. However, the seaport's interest declined and any future cooperation is dependent on the decision of the terminal operator. So far, the dryport has received 30% support for infrastructure investment from the Swedish central government, for saving CO_2 emissions, and €1 million of co-financing from the Swedish Rail Authority.

The area has been designed based on future expansion and demands. The total investment plan for new rail infrastructure, signalling systems, electricity and connection to the main line is estimated at SEK32.5 million (€3.5 million). Additionally, investments in road, water and drainage and other infrastructure are necessary and partly already made.

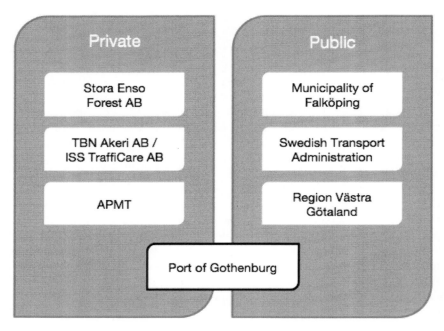

Figure 21: *Private – Public Overview Gothenburg/Falköping*

The area is located far from residential areas. The municipality has bought all necessary land for the logistics area to minimise conflicts with residents. However, other conflicts with residents might occur later when traffic increases and businesses expand. For example, three to four train arrivals could generate up to 400 truck movements per day, bringing noise, pollution and longer timber trucks in an area where there are only one-lane roads. Moreover, for effective use, the terminal would need 24-hour lighting, which could affect the environment and some nearby residents.

The direct involvement of citizens is limited. However, the municipality tries to keep conflicts low through public information campaigns. For instance, there was a conflict regarding regional environment. The municipality reacted with a public strategy: "The establishment of this Dryport gives more environmental problems locally but saves the environment globally" is how it explained the project connection with its own energy and environmental plans. The municipality has also conducted a study for environmental certification of the terminal itself and intends to develop the new logistics area with a strong environmental aspect. A continuous dialogue with private actors and citizens has been carried out during this process in order to ensure final efficiency and productivity of the area and its terminals.

Socio-economic and political effects

Because the maritime share (container transport to and from the seaport) of Skaraborg is still small at present, the socio-economic impacts of "dryport functions" are very limited. The dryport is looking into establishing companies at the 70-hectare logistics park. This is still at an early stage but there is hope that the local economy will get some benefit. The main objective for the municipality in establishing the dryport is business development and job creation. Presuming that development will progress, there will be influences on the local labour market – for instance, a higher degree of jobs in the logistics field. A two-year adult education scheme has already been started within the field of logistics. There are also plans for new educational courses to support warehouse handling.

Conclusion

The Skaraborg Logistics Centre and the Port of Gothenburg have only a very loose connection. While the seaport does not need a near dryport at the moment, the dryport depends on the seaport for export/import traffic. However, it is conceivable that it could become part of the inland network of its former container terminal operator and, with the prospect of a more efficient railway connection to continental Europe, competition between seaports could be stepped up, which would also increase the importance of inland terminals.

In contrast to the situation in Zeebrugge or Bremen, it is clear that the interests of the seaport and the dryport differ at present.

2.3 Felixstowe – Haven Gateway

Description and development

The Haven Gateway Partnership (HGP) is located in the East of England and consists of public authorities and private companies in that region, among them the ports of Felixstowe, Ipswich, Harwich International and others, which form the UK's most important gateway for container ships. The Haven Gateway Partnership is a platform for cooperation and economic promotion in the East of England.

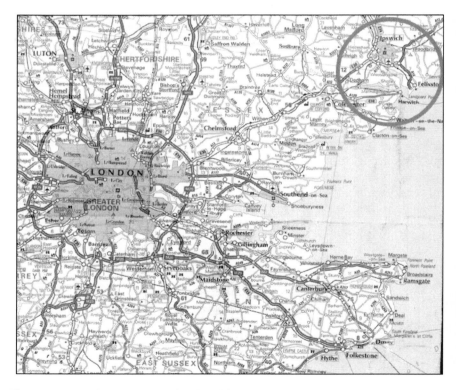

Figure 22: *Haven Gateway Partnership (HGP) location*

The most important container port relevant for dryport connections is the Port of Felixstowe. The other ports in the region are big in bulks and breakbulks (Ipswich) and passengers and cruise (Harwich International). For the dryport development, this study focuses on container ports. Felixstowe is the UK's largest container port, with throughput of 3.4 million TEU in 2010, far ahead of Southampton, with 1.5 million TEU. Situated in the South East of the UK, close to the main shipping channels, Felixstowe can serve the largest container vessels in the world without tidal restrictions.

All terminals at the Port of Felixstowe are operated by Hutchison Ports UK[26] and are open to any shipping/logistics company. The Felixstowe South Reconfiguration (phase one was completed in 2011) has provided an additional deepwater container terminal.

Two possible dryport sites have been identified by the local authorities in the district of Babergh, within close reach of Felixstowe and the other Haven Gateway ports.

The first potential dryport area is a former British Sugar site at Sproughton on the edge of Ipswich. This site has a total area of developable land of 36 hectares and its own access to the A14 motorway.

The second possible site identified is at the Brantham Industrial Area, near Manningtree. The railway line runs right alongside the site, which offers a total area of developable land of 20 hectares.

---

26   Hutchison Port Holdings is a private holding company incorporated in British Virgin Islands, it is the subsidiary of Hutchison Whampoa. In April 2006 Hutchison Whampoa sold 20% shares to PSA International, Hutchison Whampoa still owned 80%. In 2006, HPH wass the largest port operator in the world, which APM Terminals is the 2nd, and PSA International is the 3rd, according to "Annual Review of Global Container Terminal Operators 2006" published by Drewry Shipping Consultants.

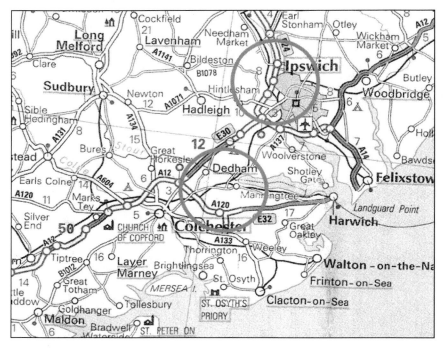

Figure 23: *Locations of the potential dryport developments*

The Port of Felixstowe operates two rail terminals, with 58 incoming and outgoing trains per day. To complement the extension of port capacity in the Felixstowe South Reconfiguration, a third rail terminal is being built. Jointly, these three terminals are planned to achieve a rail modal share of 26% of annual container traffic through the port by 2020.

The rail terminals of the Port of Felixstowe are connected to the hinterland by the Felixstowe branch line, from Felixstowe to Ipswich. The branch line is owned by Network Rail, the UK's rail network company. To carry the expected growing volumes of container traffic to/from the port, the Felixstowe to Nuneaton development (F2N) is planned. This will include the upgrading of the rail connection to allow the transport of 9ft 6in "high cube" containers and the dualling of a 4.25 mile stretch on this route. The development will ultimately allow up to 56 freight trains per day to run in both directions.

The main road connections from the Port of Felixstowe are via the A14 to Ipswich and on to the Midlands and further north, or to London via the A12.

Function and market situation

With its container terminals already handling more than 3 million TEU per year, Felixstowe is the largest container port in the UK – and further expansion is planned. The first phase of expansion has provided 1,285 metres of quay with depth alongside of 16 metres and a total area of 35.9 hectares. When phase two of this new terminal is built, total container capacity at the port will increase to 5.2 million TEU per year.

Felixstowe reports that it has no shortage of capacity inside the port and thus has no need or interest in investing in a nearby dryport to shift containers to external areas. Since the eventual dryport considered by Babergh District Council would be located relatively nearby, the function for a market extension also does not apply here. Quite the contrary – during the interview conducted at the port, we were informed that Felixstowe Port is working quite comfortably with the 17 inland destinations (by rail) for import cargo. Like most other UK ports, Felixstowe is mainly an import port. Its principal consignees are in the Greater London area, the Midlands and Northern UK[27].

The initial owners of the potential dryport area in Sproughton had intended to create residential housing at the site, with residential development providing higher profits for investors than employment-related areas. However, the district council recognised a shortage of jobs and wanted to retain the area as an industrial park or other employment-related area. Therefore, the council was seeking potential investors in port-related businesses to establish a dryport on the site. The council had been looking for potential investors dealing with port-related activities, e.g. logistics companies – but, except for Mediterranean Shipping Co. (MSC), no significant feedback was received.

Being within a near distance of the seaport, the dryport could be used by shipping companies or related companies for additional container handling, distribution, packing, or other services. The investing companies could add value by offering reduced costs compared with the same services within the seaport.

In 2006, the council contacted different potential investors in the site at Sproughton, and MSC (which has its UK headquarters just outside Ipswich) expressed commercial interest in a container drop usage. The space at the dryport

---

27   See: Garret, Mike; Latest trends in global trade and the business case for Port Centric Logistics, presentation for PortCentric Logistics conference, Birmignham March 2011.

might be cheaper than using space at the port. However, MSC has not invested since.

The Sproughton site is located near the port and is directly connected to the highway, so additional truck traffic would not greatly affect the neighbourhood. The Brantham site is situated within a mile of Manningtree railway station, offering fast and frequent passenger services to London. The site is split in two by the railway line. Both sites are "brownfield" areas which have been used for industrial purposes before. Therefore any interference with previously untouched natural environment would be very limited. One problem is that the land at both sites is contaminated by extensive industrial use in the past and would need some costly restoration.

Another problem is ownership. The Brantham site has multiple owners. The dryport site in Sproughton is even more complicated. In 2006, it was owned by private investors – but they went bankrupt at the beginning of the housing crisis in the UK (2008). Due to the following financial crisis, the subsequent owner of the site has also faced difficulties and at the moment it is unclear who actually owns the Sproughton site (date of information: May 2011). Until now, apart from the initial MSC interest, no concrete action has been taken.

Governance

The Port of Felixstowe is leased and operated by the Felixstowe Dock and Railway Company, which is owned by Hutchison Ports UK, part of the Hutchison Port Holdings Group. Much of the land on which the port is built is owned by Trinity College, Cambridge.

The policy of the port is that containers outside the port area are also outside of Hutchison's responsibility and should be dealt with by the market. Therefore, Hutchison is not interested in investing in a nearby dryport. However, it would cooperate with partners inland to improve necessary links for container shuttles into certain areas.

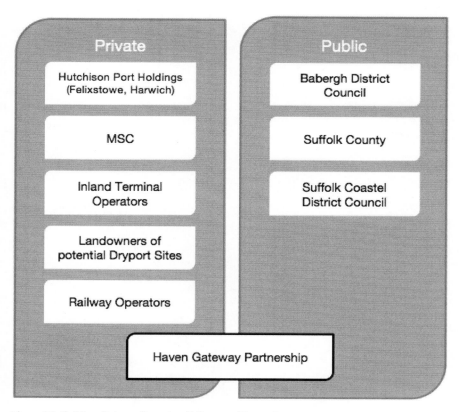

Figure 24: *Public – Private Overview Felixstowe/Haven Gateway*

The Port of Felixstowe has also agreed to invest in double-tracking the railway line from Felixstowe to Ipswich, in return for permission to extend the port. This condition was set by the national transport administration. In the UK, the Modal Shift Revenue Support scheme (MSRS) gives grant support for shifting to rail. It is designed for rail, not for coastal shipments.

The initially discussed dryport has no operator yet. Babergh District Council is the driving force but relies on private investors for the dryport development. The other district council, in whose area Felixstowe Port is located, is Suffolk Coastal.

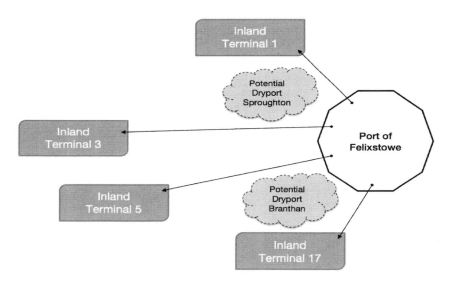

Figure 25: *Port of Felixstowe – hinterland network (independent inland terminals)*

Socio-economic and political effects

There is no railway connection to the site in Sproughton, so the only transport mode would be by road. On the transit road between Felixstowe and Ipswich, the main bottleneck is a national bridge which has to be closed during high winds. When the bridge cannot be used, lorries queue or try to find their way around, which also means a difficult traffic situation for the town of Ipswich.

Potential conflicts could also arise over the increase in lorry traffic between the site and the Port of Felixstowe when a dryport is in place. On the other hand, this could supply more jobs for lorry drivers and also employ more people on the dryport site.

Additionally, decontamination of the site is needed, which would improve the environmental situation.

There is an open and transparent process in relation to the railway planning between Felixstowe and Ipswich, which is guaranteed by the Transport Works Act order. The local authorities try to achieve a planning consensus by involving an independent judge who takes in enquiries from different stakeholders and gives recommendations to the planning inspector.

There is no modal shift with the dryport in Sproughton. An additional rail line would not be profitable because it is too nearby, so the costs for shunting are too high. While the road has bottlenecks such as the river bridge between Felixstowe and Ipswich and the entrance to the Port of Felixstowe, the single rail track to Ipswich has been another one. Rail transport could increase after the investment in another track, but this would only favour middle or long-distance dryports.

The ports and logistics sector in the Haven Gateway region handles about a third of the UK's container throughput. It creates around 32,000 jobs and generates a total turnover of about £3 billion a year. These numbers are is set to increase during the planned further development of the ports. Wages in this sector are about 20% above the regional average.

Conclusions

The initiative for the described dryport developments in Babergh District Council is politically motivated. The other partners in the Haven Gateway have no need for and no interest in a nearby dryport. A dryport development might be possible when logistics' companies can be found for investing in a container drop and additional services site with a better cost-benefit relation than in the seaport.

2.4 Zeebrugge

Description and development

Planning for the Port of Zeebrugge was started in the late 19th century by the City of Bruges, with the Belgian parliament voting in 1894 for the law approving the construction of *Port of Heyst*, later known as Port of Zeebrugge. From the creation of the first navigable channels from Bruges to the North Sea, to the rise of the flourishing economic and cultural centre in the late Middle Ages, to the decline from the 15th century onwards, the history of Bruges was closely linked to the existence or silting of navigable waterway routes facilitating trade for this Flemish region.

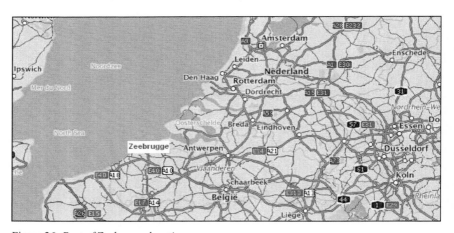

Figure 26: *Port of Zeebrugge location*

At the beginning of the 20th century, Bruges was again connected with the sea; the Port of Zeebrugge was inaugurated in 1907 by King Leopold II. But the real return to the international scene only came as a result of the comprehensive port expansion between 1970 and 1985. As a result, total cargo traffic tripled from 14 million tonnes in 1985 to 45 million tonnes in 2009.

The Port of Zeebrugge is one of the fastest growing ports in the Hamburg-Le Havre range. Zeebrugge has become, in barely a couple of decades, one of the most important entry ports for the European market[28]. There is a regional cooperation with the ports of Ostend and Antwerp.

---

28   http://www.portofzeebrugge.be/en/node/417.

In combination with a wide range of intercontinental services and good hinterland connections, extending to the North of Spain and as far as Northern Italy, Zeebrugge is well suited for international companies to organise their European or worldwide distribution. In the meantime, quite a few companies have invested in logistics centres. From here they add value to their cargo before distributing throughout Europe.

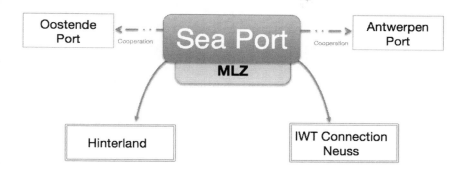

Figure 27: *Zeebrugge connections*

Zeebrugge has grown from a pure transit port to a logistics platform. In 2010, the port handled 2.5 million TEU, almost tripling its container turnover in ten years. The role of Zeebrugge as engine of the regional economy is growing. Today, 28,000 people have a job, directly or indirectly, in the port economy and related services.

It is in this context that the Maritime Logistics Zone (MLZ) at the Port of Zeebrugge is being regarded in this case study. The 120-hectare MLZ was set up in its present structure in 2009. It is directly attached to the seaport of Zeebrugge. The distance to the Port of Antwerp is approximately 136 kilometres.[29] There are direct rail and inland waterway links between the Port of Zeebrugge and the Port of Antwerp. The MLZ has a direct rail terminal, whereas cargo for inland barges has to be transhipped by lorry from the seaport. The first company starting operations at the MLZ was a coffee merchant which set up its Seabridge Logistics Centre for the handling and distribution of green coffee in 2009.

---

29   See: http://www.maritimeeconomics.com/system/files/downloads/Thesis_Stroman_
      public.pdf.

Close Dry Port

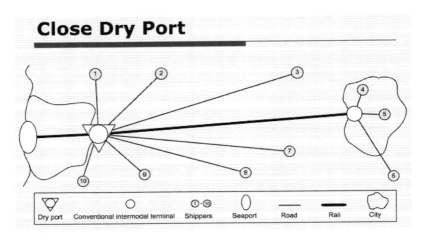

Figure 28: *Close Dry Port*

Compared with the other dryports in this study, and following the definition provided in the introduction, MLZ goes even beyond what Roso et.al. describe as a "close-by-dryport". The MLZ is located directly on the land managed by the Zeebrugge Port Authority as shown on the Zeebrugge Port Map on page 46. One could say that the Zeebrugge MLZ comes from a geographical point of view closer to a classic "packing centre" as used in many seaports in the 1970s when LCL goods were packed for the upcoming standard containers. These packing and distribution centres were very often on the seaport premises inside the customs area.

The functional analysis of the MLZ, as described below, differs substantially from those packing centres of 30-40 years ago, as the MLZ concept hosts companies for the distribution of goods (tyres), and processing and packing into consumer units (coffee and fruit juice). With increasing individual lorry transport since the 1980s as part of the emerging intermodal transport system[30], the packing of LCL cargo has often moved closer to the shippers' location, as found across the country, and in so-called "distant dryports". The companies or business within the (functional) dryport MLZ may not necessarily be located in the indicated zone of the MLZ, as the "area" has been extended to include further actors like the Toyota distribution centre and the Tropicana juice factory, which are located outside the MLZ.

---

30   See: UNESCAP Transport Division; Commercial Development of Regional Ports as Logistics Centres; Bangkok 2002, P. 20.

The MLZ extends over the purple and grey areas on the southern periphery of the port zone, marked here with a red circle:[31]

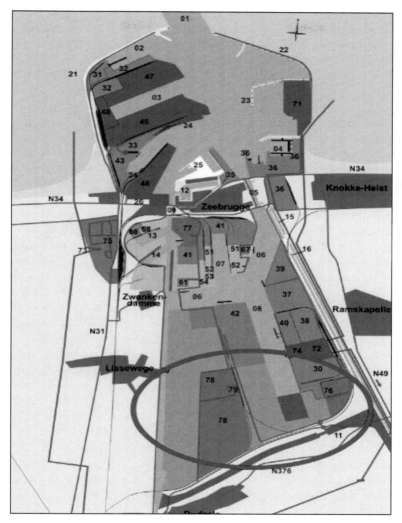

Figure 29: *Port of Zeebrugge, Map of the entire port*

---

31   http://www.portofzeebrugge.be.

Function and market situation

The MLZ is directly attached to the Port of Zeebrugge. Its development is driven by the port authority. For the seaport it serves a double function; it provides additional capacity for logistics and value-added service activities at Zeebrugge and at the same time it supports the cooperation between the ports of Zeebrugge and Antwerp. The fast rail connection between the ports of Antwerp and Zeebrugge/MLZ offers shippers the opportunity to ship their goods via Antwerp and facilitate their value-added services at MLZ. The landlord of MLZ is Zeebrugge Port Authority. As in the port itself, the land is leased to private operators.

Outstanding features are the proximity to a seaport with sufficient draft for large vessels free of tidal restrictions, clean surroundings for "green logistics", apparently good labour relations and availability of a skilled workforce, financial backing and management integration with the seaport. Around 400 companies are active in the port area of Zeebrugge and Bruges[32], realising an added value of €1,655.1 million in 2009.

The attraction of value-added services is of particular importance for Zeebrugge and the region with a view to the labour market. As there is no major industry established in the region, this is an effective way of creating jobs and generating tax revenue. The cooperation with the Port of Antwerp is aimed at creating synergies to keep up with global competition, especially with German ports. The MLZ was set up by the port authority MBZ (owned by the City of Bruges) to develop additional capacities for the handling of cargo, particularly targeting handling companies requiring clean environmental conditions, especially the food sector. Hence "green logistics" is one key selling proposition of MLZ activities.

The MLZ provides at the same time a relief function for the seaport of Zeebrugge and it creates space for additional logistics activities. The special focus of activities at MLZ is green logistics. Operations are deemed to be environmentally and climate-friendly. The companies based in the areas 76, 78 and 79 are distribution and processing facilities either requiring relatively "clean air" (e.g. coffee processing or fruit juice bottling) or being low-emission services (e.g. tyre distribution).

Seabridge Logistics is implementing this approach, with its energy-efficient warehouse significantly exceeding national and European standards for energy efficiency.

---

32   http://www.portofzeebrugge.be/en/node/502.

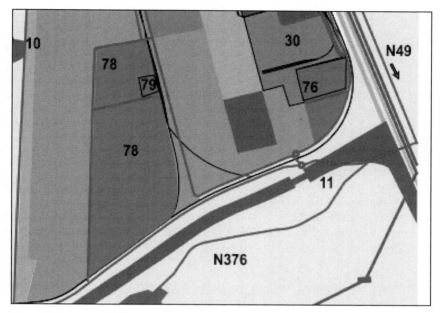

Figure 30: *Location of MLZ in the Zeebrugge Port Area (see figure 29)*

By facilitating these value-added services, MLZ is also aiming to increase local economic activity beyond core logistics processes. Value-added logistics services are particularly important for Zeebrugge and the surrounding region, as there are no major industry clusters established in the area. Logistics are the main source of jobs and tax revenue.

Another aspect of the close linkages between the Port of Zeebrugge and MLZ is the improvement of hinterland connections in order to expand the customer area and reach further clientele. There are currently severe restrictions particularly in the inland waterway connection towards France. Their removal could potentially significantly improve the competitiveness of Zeebrugge.

In addition, MLZ contributes to and forms part of the cooperation between the ports of Zeebrugge and Antwerp. This is aimed at strengthening each other's competitive market position by creating synergies. The first example of this co-operation is the operation of Seabridge Logistics, the first company to establish a subsidiary at MLZ. The coffee handled by Seabridge Logistics at MLZ is imported via Antwerp and then shipped on special trains to MLZ Zeebrugge. The main reason for this is the shortage of suitable land at Antwerp and availability of the same at Zeebrugge. Through this cooperation, Antwerp can prevent losing overseas services to other ports and, at the same time, Zeebrugge attracts new business and generates additional jobs and tax revenue.

The target regions of MLZ or regional cargo destinations of Zeebrugge are not found in the direct geographic proximity and therefore cannot be called classic "hinterland" places of the seaport. The business focus areas of MLZ are found in Western Germany, UK East Coast, Southern Sweden, Northern France, Luxemburg, Italy, Northern Spain and South East Europe. These are mainly reached by rail and road, with only a minor share of inland navigation. Shortsea and feeder connections are in place to Scandinavia, UK and the Iberian Peninsula.

The connections to North France could potentially be improved through the implementation of plans for the Seine-Schelde-West inland navigation project. This long-term infrastructure project is aimed at the construction of a new channel connecting the Seine and Scheldt rivers. This channel could accommodate inland barges of up to 300 TEU. The Minister of Public Works has to decide on the realisation of the plans.

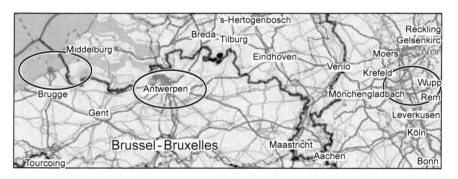

Figure 31: *Ports of Zeebrugge, Antwerp and Neuss/ Germany (marked with red circles)*

Governance

The Port Authority of Zeebrugge is the Maatschappij van de Brugse Zeevaar-tinrichtingen N.V. (MBZ), set up in 1895 as a joint venture of the City of Bruges and private investors. Its main shareholder is the City of Bruges. This ownership allows the local (and indirectly the Flemish) government to maintain some influence in the development of the port. However, actual operations are undertaken by private companies to whom port land is leased by MBZ.

The interests of the private companies active at Zeebrugge are represented through the Association Port of Zeebrugge Interests (APZI), founded in 1973. Currently around 130 companies are affiliated to APZI. These include shipping companies, shipping agents, forwarding agents and transport companies, as well as trade, industry and service companies. Local leaseholders contribute to these aims, pursuing their own commercial interests by setting up additional storage and handling capacities to relieve the(ir) facilities at the Port of Antwerp. This attracts additional cargo to Zeebrugge and generates value-added services that contribute to an increase of the local share of the logistics chain. At the same time, the Seabridge Logistics warehouse is in line with the environmental and climate goals of MBZ, as it is one of the most energy-efficient warehouses in Europe.

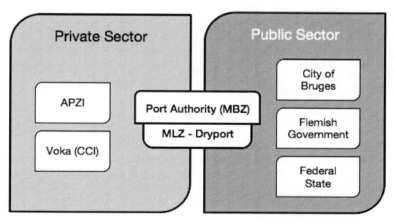

Figure 32: *Governance scheme in Zeebrugge Port: private sector bodies and public sector actors*

Cooperation in the development of the port is therefore mainly a matter of consultations between MBZ and APZI. This cooperation ensures that the political aims of the government and the economic interests of the private sector are brought together in the development of the port. The Chamber of Commerce and Industry (VOKA) supports the development of the Port of Zeebrugge and the MLZ. Chamber membership in the Province of West Flanders covers approximately 3,400 companies, representing two-thirds of regional employment. Involvement with port and logistics affairs is mainly pursued via networking with APZI, cooperation in the Alliance Zeebrugge-Antwerp and the provision of services such the organisation of B2B events or dedicated projects.

Infrastructure investment decisions are the responsibility of the Flemish Government, which puts a special emphasis on port economics and a transport-logistics strategy for the area Zeebrugge-Ostend with its maritime and airport infrastructures. "Flanders Port Area", forging the cooperation between the Belgian seaports, is a network initiative of the Flemish Government within the "Flanders in Action 2020" initiative[33]. Flanders Port Area puts a special focus on training, employees' skills and a broad knowledge base.

The Port of Zeebrugge is an "economic engine" of Zeebrugge and the region. There are neither significant industrial clusters nor traditional (heavy) industries based in the area. Therefore, the political aims and economic interests of port-related businesses converge to a large extent. It is in the government's interests to attract logistics activities and in particular value-added services with a significant effect on labour market and tax revenue. On the other hand, private companies active in and around the port are interested in attractive framework conditions for their business. Being organised in the APZI, the private sector has an effective platform for dealing with the local government.

Socio-economic and political effects

The modal split at the Port of Zeebrugge is 52% road, 16% rail, 16% transshipment, 11% pipelines, 1% inland navigation, 5% estuary barges. The general aim is to shift more cargo to rail and inland waterways. A major deficit in the hinterland connection is the restricted access to European inland waterways. This is the reason for the estuary barge service from the Port of Zeebrugge into the river Scheldt and on to Antwerp and German destinations on the Rhine such as Duisburg and Neuss.

The coffee transported from Antwerp to Zeebrugge is carried on a regular rail shuttle. As both Antwerp and Zeebrugge have a good rail infrastructure,

---

33   See: http://www.flandersportarea.be.

transport via rail in this respect is competitive with road transport, despite the unusually short distance. The distance of the rail connection is just exceeding the minimum distance for rail transport to be eligible for state subsidies. Although rail is generally regarded as a means of transport for long distances, in this case it is also economically feasible for the shorter distance.

As the MLZ is relatively small compared to the size of the Port of Zeebrugge, no significant changes of the overall economic situation of the region are to be expected. Nevertheless the MLZ will contribute to further growth of the port-related economy in Zeebrugge and the region. Additional investments are set to be attracted by the MLZ. The clear profile with a focus on environmentally friendly services and energy efficiency creates a selling proposition, which makes the MLZ particularly attractive for companies from relevant sectors, e.g. the food industry.

The Port of Zeebrugge is the key employer in the region. As there is no single large industry in the region, the labour market depends heavily on SMEs and the port (28,000 jobs in the port alone.[34] As the MLZ contributes to further growth of the Port of Zeebrugge, it could be expected to have a positive effect, especially because it is aimed at attracting value-added services with a view to increasing local employment. The scale of this effect will, though, be restricted due to the relatively restricted size of the MLZ. Also, no significant change in salary levels is expected as a result of it.

The costs for the MBZ are related to the development of the dryport area and set-up of related infrastructure. The benefit in turn is the attraction of cargo and value-added services. The public takes advantage of increased local economic activity, resulting in generation of jobs and tax revenue.

The private companies investing in the MLZ have to carry the cost of land lease and construction of their facilities (suprastructure). In turn, they take advantage of the provided infrastructure and nearby access to the port.

Conclusions

The clear focus on logistics functions of the Port of Zeebrugge since its construction, not being primarily part of the supply chain for heavy industries[35], reinforced by the investments since the 1970s, has likely facilitated a mixed economic pattern. This variety of commercial aspects allows relatively independent

---

34   http://www.portofzeebrugge.be/en/node/500.

35   Other ports, such as Gijon/Spain and some Welsh ports have formerly been conceived primarily as installations for heavy industries like shipbuilding, energy production, steel factories or shipping of raw materials. This dependence was often evident also for inland ports attached to industry basis like Liège, Duisburg, etc.

political decision-making by the port authority and the economic actors, neither being immediately dependent on changing global production patterns, like many other ports, nor on the City of Bruges as its main shareholder. However, economic and political turmoil such as trade changes and wars have affected Zeebrugge as well.

The recent focus on "green logistics" at the dryport not only attracts investments and long-term lease contracts, but also facilitates cooperation with the neighbouring Port of Antwerp, to mutual benefit, and generates cargo for the seaport.

The complex and developed networking capability of the port cluster is, in our view, a factor contributing highly to the competitiveness of Zeebrugge Port and may sustain this position on a durable basis. Regulations and perceived conflicts of use are resolved for both for the seaport and dryport and there are stable labour relations. Together with the envisaged and operational hinterland links, Zeebrugge appears a modern port as regards the infra- and suprastructure, diversity of economic operation and governance patterns.

3 Comparing the Cases: Conflicts and Contradictions

The first step of the cross-case analysis focuses the main research hypotheses of the study and identifies similarities of and differences between the processes of dryport integration at Bremen/Bremerhaven, Gothenburg/Falköping, Haven Gateway and Zeebrugge. At the beginning of our empirical survey and consequently of this report, we referred to different dimensions of the dryport concept as the spatial, economic and functional dimensions, as well as to the dimension of governance. These different dimensions will be applied in the subsequent description of the interfaces and the characteristic differences that emerged from the case studies.

3.1 Integration of Locational and Economic Elements

Summarising the spatial, economic and functional dimensions of the dryport concept, we can systematically identify different combinations of these functions showing how different types of logistic hubs are embedded into respective logistic chains and how they are connected with a seaport. In general, we can distinguish between *four types of dryport:*

- *Dryports as a part of "extended gateways"* (main ports and/or port clusters with nearby freight villages, value-added services, distribution functions, etc.). Decisive in this context is that this function is performed by the entire region, not only by one port[36]. An "extended gateway" would include, for example, the combination Antwerp-Zeebrugge-Zeebrugge Maritime Logistic Zone (possibly also including Ostend); or the port cluster Bremerhaven-Wilhelmshaven-Bremen including the GVZ und Neustadt Port.
- *Dryports as a "functional satellite"* (as "subsidiary" or "external office" related to one or more seaports). The dryport can have either a close or a more distant geographical location. The *functional* component is important here. These "satellites" can either be part of the company group or contracted units. Depending on their size and economic independence from the seaport operator(s), these "satellites" may serve as a complementary partner but also

---

36 Charlier, J.J. 2011: Hinterlands, Port Regionalisation and Extended Gateways: The case of Belgium and Northern France. In: Hall et.al. (eds.): Integrating Seaports and Trade Corridors. Farnham,UK/Burlington,VT (Ashgate).

work as a competitor for the seaport; not least, the dryport could constitute a competitive advantage for other competing seaports. (For example, in the case of Duisburg Port, both Rotterdam and Antwerp want to gain as much as possible control over the Port of Duisburg because this would improve their individual market position considerably; therefore, each of them is interested in buying shares in Duisburg from the German government holding.)

• *Dryports as hinterland hubs* (which primarily serve to gain and provide access to larger (metropolitan) areas, important industrial districts and/or specific, geographically limited markets (hub-and-spoke-model)). In this context, the dryport is rather a handling hub (distribution park, freight village or similar) connecting the seaport with certain markets or clients. The latter function serves also to "bind" a client to the respective seaport. An example is the Falköping dryport in relation to Gothenburg seaport. Falköping would use its function as a "dryport" to Gothenburg (or another port) if there were to be a regular container shuttle with respective volume. However, at present the market access offered by Falköping is for economic reasons only of minor interest to the Port of Gothenburg. This is why a considerable relief function cannot be fulfilled by the Skaraborg Logistic Centre and it is the reason why Falköping acts on its own, mainly with the timber business. Further examples in this logic are the contract partners of the Eurogate network in hinterland regions or joint ventures.

• Exclusive *multimodal cargo terminals*, which provide handling and transshipment functions for moving goods from road to rail, for example, and which only to a very limited extent take over a nodal connection or functionality. Those installations can hardly be referred to as dryports (this situation applies, for example, to Falköping without the dryport shuttle in use). This example demonstrates very clearly the significance of railroad or other transport operators for the function of a dryport; if there is no direct physical connection to the seaport or if this connection cannot be operated profitably, then there is no integration of the dryport into the logistics chain, even if the seaport and the dryport are interested in that. The question of economic conditions for transport operations is, of course, also relevant for dryports serving as hinterland hubs or as functional satellites.

In reality, the majority of existing dryports seems to represent a combination of the types a, b and c, and many different variations could be found. But one of the characteristics of major importance appears to be the issue of *entrepreneurial control*, which means that the main drivers of establishing and operating a dryport will determine the different kinds of entrepreneurial control:

Table 1: Main drivers for dryports

	Bremerhaven/ Bremen	Gothenburg/ Falköping	Haven Gateway/ Babergh	Zeebrugge
Port Authorities				X
Terminal Operators of Seaport	X			
Terminal Operators Inland		X		
Public Authorities / Municipalities	X	X	X	X
Freight Forwarders / Logistics companies	X	X		X

The nature of the "driver", more public or more private, correlates with the market situation of the seaport, as shown in the table. The main driving force in seaports with a highly competitive environment is to provide an additional service, also via a dryport, to their customers in order to continue attracting cargo to the seaport facilities.

In the cases of Gothenburg/Falköping and Felixstowe, the interest in developing the dryport stems rather from inland-based municipalities seeking prospects in their region. These two seaports have no or only minor interest in being involved in inland terminal development, as neither face serious competition from other seaports. In contrast with these two cases, Bremen/Bremerhaven in North Germany and Zeebrugge in Belgium are trying hard to compete successfully with other seaports on the north-western range:

Table 2: Competition between Seaports

	Bremerhaven/ Bremen	Gothenburg/ Falköping	Haven Gateway/ Babergh	Zeebrugge
Position of seaport compared to other seaports	High Competition	Low Competition	Low Competition	High Competition

In the case of *Gothenburg/Falköping*, the seaport, the terminal and the railway operator are companies in their own right and not interlinked. Hence Falköping is an independent entity relying strongly on the other stakeholders for its dryport function.

Felixstowe as a privately owned and managed seaport does not seem to have an economic interest in a dryport in the *Haven Gateway* area. The economic function or interest of the port operator is limited to the port operation itself; the further distribution is left to other operators. Limited engagement is found in ensuring access to and from the port, but no engagement in further handling operations was found.

In *Bremen/Bremerhaven*, the dominant stakeholders BLG and Eurogate endeavour to control the logistics chains as much as possible, with the aim to be able to decide themselves which cargo can be moved when, how and where.

This requires a large extent of internal coordination and cooperation and relates strongly to the set of an "extended gateway", which holds strong potential for developing dryport functions near to the seaport. But extending the control over logistics chains as a strategic goal is also the reason for the installation of a network of owned or contracted hinterland hubs.

Zeebrugge is seen in a similar dynamic as Bremen/Bremerhaven and develops its own dryport capacities, which connect Zeebrugge with own (controlled) transport links and rolling stock. The environment is less complex than in Bremen-Bremerhaven and thus allows quicker and swifter developments.

To sum up the spatial/economic/functional dimension of dryports:

The strongly expressed *Conditions for Demand* (Porter)[37] by "difficult" clients (pushing the firm to provide innovations) are decisive for any success of a dryport.

In the case of *Zeebrugge*, both the competitive situation in the Northern Range and the vicinity with Antwerp regarding the port dimension but also the thrust to "generate its own industry" (or its own "hinterland") have led to a situation in which Zeebrugge Port is offering both new (innovative) harbour services and development of its own hinterland by creating an exclusive commercial zone in the port area (MLZ).

A similar situation can be described for *Bremen/Bremerhaven* companies, which are demanding public intervention for ensuring the continuing competitive location of the dryport the GVZ, as well as considering the residents' interests to keep the planned/working dryport area liveable for them.

This "private" demand side appears to be very low to non-existent in the *Felixstowe-Haven Gateway* dryport discussion and only of little relevance for *Gothenburg/Falköping*, which is (as it seems) mainly stimulated by the respective municipalities.

---

37   According to Porter, one condition for success is to have "difficult" or demanding clients, which push the firm to provide innovations. See: Porter, M. E., The Competitive Advantage of Nations, New York, 1990.

3.2 Governance Solutions

The process of planning, launching and operating a dryport is or at least should be embedded into the process of integration and implementation of the involved stakeholders. Stakeholders include not only economic actors such as forwarders, shipping companies, truck owners and other clients, but also public administration on local, regional and national level and residents, too.

This coordination and sometimes conflict-solving tasks will primarily be given to and fulfilled by the different bodies of the public administration, here shortly named as "state"[38]. The role of the state in planning, launching and operating a dryport depends very much on the status of the operator of the respective dryport:

Table 3: Public or private operator for each dryport

	Bremen / Inland Terminals	Falköping	Haven Gateway / Babergh	Zeebrugge
Landlord	Bremenports (Regional Ministry)	Municipality	Private Consortium	Port of Zeebrugge (City)
Operator (Public)	Neustädter Hafen: BLG/ Eurogate, Weserport etc.			
Operator (Private)	The GVZ: Different logistics companies	TBN Akeri A/B Initially: ISS TraffiCare, Sweden	MSC, Several private operators (seaport Felixstowe)	Different concession holders like APMT, etc.

UK/Haven Gateway/Babergh case study: Local politicians were using to a certain extent the "dryport" concept in the Babergh district for their aims regarding a specific site. It is questionable whether the initial intention was at all to create a dryport; in any case, it has not yet been achieved. The stated aim to keep the site free of private housing interests was, however, achieved. Hence, we could not find any conflict of interest with the commercial port actors; the Haven Gateway cooperation seems to develop well. Larger regional or national political interests did not seem to be of importance.

---

38   "State" here represents public authorities, at local, regional, national and European level. The "state" can be, for example, transport ministries, port authorities (except for the UK) and also agencies or companies held 100% by other public bodies.

In the *Sweden/Gothenburg-Falköping case*, the drive to establish a dryport was a successful political initiative which, however, due to low commercial interest or impact, has not yet led to a fully functioning dryport. Moreover, the Falköping case may be only seemingly "state driven"; in reality, its economic success depends on the private interests of the companies on the dryport operators side and also of the companies from the linked seaport, i.e. Gothenburg. The dryport needs a sufficient amount of container volume to function successfully. If the seaport does not have the strategic interest in the dryport, it may even happen that the dryport itself becomes a competitor to the seaport with its ambitions to become a dryport for the Port of Hamburg after the Fehmarn-Belt-Link has been built.

For the *German situation/the Bremen-Bremerhaven case*, we can see the state acting as "facilitator"; public bodies support both the port community and the logistic operators to have an environment in which they can cooperate and establish commercial cases. Those public actors are relatively influential and they can take over a mediator's role in conflicts between commercial interests and those of the residents (see below "The process of governance").

In the *Zeebrugge case*, the state can be regarded as "entrepreneur". This is facilitated by low to zero conflicts between residents and commercial interests. Necessary mediations are conducted either by the port authority itself or by the Chamber of Commerce with its network. We could identify a transparent and clearly organised division of labour. This also seems to be true for vertical integration.

Beyond the above discussed facts and targets that Dryports should contribute to cargo-shift strategies (which are designed to take pressure off congested transport routes and terminals), the planning, implementation and operation of dryports cause a new dimension of problems in those areas, where the territorial expansion (building of the new dryport) – see the spatial dimension – takes place. Typically, there are combinations of the following problems:

- New infrastructure has to be built and in many cases the costs by far exceed public budgets;
- Those who benefit from new infrastructure differ from those who pay for them. Control (monitoring) and administrative (management) issues are in the hands of the benefiting enterprises/partners;
- There are often conflicting land use and economic interests, for example between port operators and housing or environmental concerns, but also between port business and "inland logistics business".
- Increasing legal restrictions – for example, concerning noise, environmental issues, housing, etc., lead to long planning procedures;

- The interests of growing numbers of relevant stakeholders have to be taken into account.

In every single case of "hinterland expansion" or implementation of a "dryport", all of these problems are mixed in a specific way but always need to be resolved if expansion and release strategies are to be implemented successfully and work efficiently. This means that these kinds of activities basically generate a complex *political* management problem.

Coming from this, the areas of conflict (environment, infrastructure development, volume of traffic) and the level (high, medium, low) of conflicts within these areas can be identified for the four case studies:

Table 4: Areas and level of conflicts in dryports

	Bremerhaven/ Bremen	Gothenburg/ Falköping	Haven Gateway/ Babergh	Zeebrugge
Environment	Medium	Medium	Low	Low
Infrastructure development	High	Medium	Low	High
Volume of Traffic	Medium	Medium	Medium	Low

The main potential areas of conflict in launching dryports again show a higher competitive situation for dryport locations close to seaports, which already find themselves in strong competition with other seaports. Compared to Falköping and Haven Gateway, there is a much higher potential for conflict in Bremen/Bremerhaven (new access motorway for the dryport) and Zeebrugge (major extension of an inland canal to France) for infrastructure. In conclusion, there is a close correlation between competitive seaports and infrastructure-related conflicts in the sense that establishing and operating a dryport in densely populated and industrialised areas (as in Bremen/Bremerhaven and in the Zeebrugge Canal Zone) on the one hand will lead to stronger conflicts. On the other hand, the problems and conflicts caused by a dense population and by complex business networks are forcing the development of measures and instruments for adequate governance.

There are obvious similarities between the Bremerhaven/Bremen and Zeebrugge cases (including a highly competitive environment, which is neither the case for Falköping/Gothenburg nor for Felixstowe) but the North German location is larger and the constellation of stakeholders is more complex, while the interest identified in the Belgian case is much higher than in the German one.

The complexity of the German situation may be due to strong conflicts of interest which accompany port and related infrastructure developments. The "state" cannot as easily cooperate with private interests but must also take into consideration the interests of the citizens/residents and general society. Moderated processes and round tables are found, which lead to a variety of clearing offices, coordination instruments, etc. Communication, coordination and cooperation have been recognised as important factors for the port/logistics community and hence respective instruments have been established and are being maintained.

For the Gothenburg/Falköping and Felixstowe case studies, we encountered (relatively) only a few overlapping dryport issues and consequently little respective instruments for coordination. Although there is the Haven Gateway Partnership covering Felixstowe, consisting of local public and private bodies, but without the existence of a dryport, there is no issue for coordination. In Sweden, also due to the economic crisis, the Gothenburg-Falköping link seems to be less active. Calls (from Falköping) to use the dryport for environmental reasons find little response from the seaport of Gothenburg, as no additional benefit can be identified.

The Felixstowe/Haven Gateway case study shows the variety of instruments which could have been used for infrastructure-related conflict moderation. In some local land use conflicts, a judge was installed as advisor/moderator, who seemingly can ensure that acceptable solutions are found. It can be assumed that this variation is a very lean and flexible solution to the problem of coordination and conflict management but likely it works only in an environment of limited complexity. Unfortunately this tool had been used only in a dryport-*related* process, as in the Haven Gateway case no dryport has been launched.

4 Governance and Competition as Conditions for Dryport Success

Summarising the insights into the development of dryports at four different locations, representing completely different conditions and taking into account the comparison of the four case studies, it is shown that the process of planning, implementing, building and operating a dryport is a process of multiple integration:

- *Integration into the logistics chain:* This comprises the *spatial and functional dimension* of dryports – with a special focus on the function of relieving pressure on the connected seaport. Undoubtedly the location of a dryport, as well as its functions in the logistics chain, plays a relevant role for any aspect of relief, but if there will be a considerable impact on the environment, for the mitigation of capacity problems or transport corridor congestion, it depends, at the end of the day, on business and governance models. Hence, a true and efficient relief of the seaport's capacities or of the transport connections' capacities can only be expected if the other integrations are realised too.
- *Integration into single companies' strategies:* This comprises the *economic dimension* of dryports – with special focus on the entrepreneurial control of the logistics chain by the main economic actors. The relationship between seaport and dryport can be organised in many different ways but the closer the ties are – through a common management, for instance – the better the chances are of implementing a coordinated cooperation between seaport and dryport and of making the dryport an integrated part of an extended gateway.
- *Integration into intra- and interregional structures:* This comprises the *governance dimension* of dryports – with special focus on the mediation between the different interests of local stakeholders, including residents or organised interest groups. This kind of conflict management and coordination is mostly organised by the state/public administration. Apart from that, the governance of company relations, networks and business clusters is a task of increasing relevance.

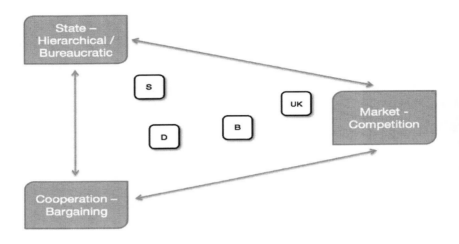

Figure 33: *Relational triangle*

If a combination of all three factors is achieved, there is a good chance that, in cooperation with the corresponding seaport, a dryport can be implemented and operate successfully. Regarding the complexity of the integration require-ments, it must be highlighted that the governance dimension is crucial to the dryport concept. Consequently, appropriate structures and institutions must be created, as the coordination of interests, decisions and actions normally does not work satisfactorily in uncoordinated self-organisation. The existence and main-tenance of those structures is an indicator of the stakeholder's commitment to the dryport issue.

Putting the four examined dryport sites into a relational triangle between state-intervention, commercial and market-driven coordination and a coopera-tion- oriented type of industrial network relations, which mainly works in the modus of "bargaining", then the *Bremen/Bremerhaven* and *Zeebrugge* cases could be found in the middle of this triangle with a clear link to networking methods, whereas the *Gothenburg/Falköping case* is very close to public inter-ests and the *Haven Gateway-Babergh case* is rather close to market coordination and commercial interests.

The comparison of the four case studies has shown clearly that successful dryport strategies are those:

- which help to integrate the dryport into a wider logistic and economic network or "extended gateway";
- whose framework is not only determined by a single mechanism for coordination or by a "traditional" mixture of state regulation and market mechanisms, but which are also coordinated by a cooperative bargaining mechanism, and
- which are considering the interests of *all* stakeholders concerned. In doing so, it could and can contribute to the optimisation of the (regional) logistics network and the functional logistic chains.

In other words: Spatial relief and environmental concerns in implementing and running a dryport do matter but, at the end of the day, competition decides. However, this does not mean that the question of "governance" is irrelevant. In particular for those cases which already have the characteristics of an "extended gateway", it is of high importance to establish a well-working mechanism for internal cooperation and coordination. "Good governance" of internal structures – including the dryport –becomes an increasingly crucial condition for the competitive position of the entire extended gateway.

References

Annual Review of Global Container Terminal Operators 2006. Published by Drewry Shipping Consultants, 2006;

Charlier, J.J.. Hinterlands, Port Regionalisation and Extended Gateways: The case of Belgium and Northern France. In: Hall et.al. (eds.): Integrating Seaports and Trade Corridors; p. 235-246. Farnham, UK/Burlington, VT (Ashgate), 2011;

Dooms, Michael. Crafting The Integrative Value Proposition For Large Scale Transport Infrastructure Hubs. A Stakeholder Management Approach, Brussels (ASP) 2010;

Dryport Conference. Intermodal Strategies for Integrating Ports & Hinterlands, Conference, 21 & 22 October 2010, Balmoral Hotel, Edinburgh;

Garret, Mike. Latest trends in global trade and the business case for Port Centric Logistics. Presentation, PortCentric Logistics conference, Birmingham March 2011;

Guy, Emmanuel; Lapointe, Frédéric. Building Value into Transport Chains: The Challenges of Multi-Goal Policies, In: Hall et.al. (eds.): Integrating Seaports and Trade Corridors; p.193-206. Farnham, UK/Burlington, VT (Ashgate), 2011;

Häkli, Jouni; Minca, Claudio. Social Capital and Urban Networks of Trust, Farnham, UK/Burlington, VT (Ashgate), 2009;

Koch, Henrike; Münch, Steffen; Nestler, Steffen; Nobel, Thomas. Ranking der europäischen GVZ-Standorte – Benchmarking der europäischen Erfahrungen. Berlin 2010;

Notteboom, Theo (ed.). Current Issues in Shipping, Ports and Logistics. Brussels (ASP) 2011;

Notteboom, Theo; Ducruet, César; Langen, Peter de (eds.). Ports in Proximity. Competition and Coordination among Adjacent Seaports, Farnham, UK/Burlington, VT (Ashgate), 2009;

Porter, M. E.; The Competitive Advantage of Nations, New York, 1990;

Roso, Violeta; Woxenius, Johan; Lumsdem, Kent. The dry port concept: connecting container seaports with the hinterland. In: Journal of Transport Geography Volume17, Issue 5, September 2009;

Roso, Violeta. Emergence and Significance of Dry Ports. Presentation, Göteborg 2008-09-05;

Roso, Violeta. Emergence and significance *of dry ports;* Report - Department of Logistics and Transportation, Chalmers University of Technology , ISSN 1652-8026, Gothenburg 2006;

Trainaviciute, Lina. StratMoS Work Package C report. In: The Dry Port - Concept and Perspectives, FDT- Association of Danish Transport and Logistics Centres, Main Author Trainaviciute, Lina, Aalborg July 2009;

UNCTAD/RDP/LDC/7. Handbook on the Management and Operation of dry ports, Geneva 1991;

UNESCAP Transport Division. Commercial Development of Regional Ports as Logistics Centres; Bangkok 2002;

Verhoeven, Patrick. ESPO 2011: European Port Governance. ESPO Fact-Finding Report, Brussels 2011.

Internet References

Bremenports website:
http://www.bremen-ports.de/

Center for Maritime Economics & Logistics website:
http://www.maritimeeconomics.com/

Deutsche GVZ-Gesellschaft mbH (DGG) website:
http://www.GVZ-org.de/

Dryport website:
http://www.dryport.org/

Dryport Conference, Edinburgh, Scotland, October 20-22, 2010 website:
http://dryport-conference.tri-napier.org/

European Sea Ports Organisation (ESPO) website:
http://www.espo.be/

Federal Ministry of Transport,
Building and Urban Development (BMVBS) website:
http://www.bmvbs.de/

Flanders Logistics website:
http://www.flandersportarea.be/

Port of Hamburg website:
http://www.hafen-hamburg.de/

Port of Zeebrugge website:
http://www.portofzeebrugge.be/

South East of Scotland transport Partnership (SEStran) website:
http://www.sestran.gov.uk/

Transport Research Institute (TRI) website:
http://www.tri.napier.ac.uk/

VIA Bremen website:
http://www.via-bremen.com/

Wirtschaftsförderung Bremen – Regional Development Agency Bremen
    website:
http://www.wfb-bremen.de

Graphics and Pictures – Index and References

Index Tables

Maritime Logistik / Maritime Logistics

Herausgegeben von Prof. Dr. Hans Dietrich Haasis, Prof. Dr. Burkhard Lemper
und Prof. Dr. Frank Arendt

Ziel dieser Schriftenreihe des *Instituts für Seeverkehrswirtschaft und Logistik (ISL)* ist es, Aspekte und Entwicklungen aus den verschiedenen Bereichen der maritimen Logistikbranchen aufzugreifen und aktuelle Trends und Perspektiven zu diskutieren. Dabei meint Maritime Logistik – Maritime Logistics nicht nur die klassischen Bereiche wie Schifffahrt, Häfen, Schiffbau oder Verkehrspolitik, sondern schließt auch die Betrachtung der vielen weiteren Akteure in den globalen Transportketten ein, die direkt oder indirekt an den Logistikprozessen der maritimen Wirtschaft beteiligt sind.

Aufgegriffen werden logistische Fragestellungen zu Themen wie z.b. Hinterlandverkehr und intermodale Verkehre, Mesologistik und regionale Netzwerke wie GVZ und Logistikzentren, nachhaltige Geschäftsmodelle und Ressourceneffizienz oder Supply Chain Controlling. Im Mittelpunkt der Reihe *Maritime Logistik – Maritime Logistics* stehen aber auch informationslogistische Themen wie die Planung und Überwachung intermodaler Transportketten durch ein aktives Supply Chain Event Management, die Sicherheit und Transparenz im internationalen Containerverkehr oder die Planungsunterstützung und Optimierung logistischer Prozesse in Häfen und Terminals mit Hilfe quantitativer Methoden.

Band 1 Burkhard Lemper / Manfred Zachcial (eds.): Trends in Container Shipping. Proceedings of the ISL Maritime Conference 2008. 9th and 10th of December, World Trade Center Bremen. 2009.

Band 2 Hans-Dietrich Haasis / Holger Kramer / Burkhard Lemper (Hrsg.): Maritime Wirtschaft – Theorie, Empirie und Politik. Festschrift zum 65. Geburtstag von Manfred Zachcial. 2010.

Band 3 Kerstin Lange: Engpassorientierte Analyse der Ver- und Entsorgungslogistik von Steinkohlekraftwerken. Unter besonderer Beachtung der maritimen Logistik. 2011.

Band 4 Torben Möller: Finanzierung von Seehafeninfrastrukturen. 2012.

Band 5 Burkhard Lemper / Thomas Pawlik / Susanne Neumann (eds.): The Human Element in Container Shipping. 2012.

Band 6 Manuel Kühn / Karsten Seidel / Jochen Tholen / Günter Warsewa: Dryports - Local Solutions for Global Transport Challenges. A Study by the Institute Labour and Economy (IAW) of the University of Bremen. 2012.

www.peterlang.de